QUALITY OF LIFE

WHAT IT REALLY REQUIRES
HOW TO GET IT AND KEEP IT

BRYAN KEMP, PH.D.

TABLE OF CONTENTS

THIS BOOK IS DEDICATED TO MY FAMILY, MY EXTENDED FAMILY, AND ALL MY FRIENDS WHO ARE INTERESTED IN HAVING A QUALITY LIFE.

INTRODUCTION

CHAPTER 1: WHAT THIS BOOK IS ALL ABOUT

Life is precious. As far as we have proof, we do not get a second chance at this glorious experiment called life. We do not get a "do-over," a "mulligan." As far as we know, there's also no other planet where life like ours occurs. We get one chance at deriving whatever we can from life and giving back to those who will follow us what we have learned about this miracle we call life. Life can be enhanced in only one of two ways; either by extending its length or by improving its quality. We have successfully increased length of life from an average of 21 years in ancient Rome to a current level of approximately 80 years. We have also improved life as far as providing more people with the benefits of technology such as the availability of clean water, electricity, and the treatment of illnesses. However, according to many experts and ample proof, we have not increased the quality of our day to day living substantially since about the 1960s. This book is concerned with how we can improve the quality of our experience of living using relatively simple and valid techniques. This book takes the reader through an examination of the most basic factors that determine both a low quality of life and a high quality of life. It is hoped that, by reading this book, more people will be able to have a life that is less distressing, more rewarding, and more like they would choose to have it.

This book describes recent advances in what we know about

quality of life or QOL, how to assess it and, more importantly, how to improve it. This book is not about how to improve your material wealth or your standing in the community. If you want to learn how to be richer, to live in a more stylish home, or get a promotion, then you should read other books. However, if you are interested in learning more about how to have a life that is fuller, more rewarding, more meaningful, and less distressing, then this book is one you will probably find useful and enjoyable. You will learn that what really determines whether we have a high quality of life or a low one is based upon the nature of our everyday experiences and whether those experiences are mostly positive or mostly negative. The term QOL has come about as a way of describing the quality of the experience of living in contrast to a measure of the quantity of things people possess or the number of activities in which they engage. It is meant to capture in some essence what makes life worth living. Most people would like to improve their quality of life, but they don't know how to go about it.

The most common source of confusion when we talk about quality of life is its distinction from a related term, Standard of Living. Standard of living is a measure of how many objective indicators of social standing a person possesses, such as whether they own a home or a car, have a certain level of income, or whether they have graduated from college. The more of these things a person has, then the higher their standing in the community or, in other words, their standard of living. However, standard of living has little to do with whether a person is happy versus discouraged, leading an enjoyable life versus an empty life, or whether they have a sense of purpose in life versus a sense of emptiness. Many or most people believe that the only way to improve one's quality of life is through improving one's standard of living or changing the objective circumstances in their life. This is not true as it is easy to see that many people with a high standard of living report a low quality of life and, contrarily, many people with apparently lower circumstances in their life report a high quality of life. Most people would like to have a high standard of living, but they also want a high quality of life. Research has shown that standard of living has increased in most industrialized nations over the last 50 years, while quality of life has remained static. The most commonly expressed reason for this difference is that most people have become focused on outward, objective signs of competitive success and material possessions, and have ignored or paid relatively less attention to the subjective, experiential factors in life that contribute to quality of living.

The experiences that contribute to one's rating of their quality of life include, at their core, three kinds of positive experiences and three kinds of negative experiences. As simple as it may seem, the relative proportion of these experiences a person has on a regular basis determines his or her quality of life. When everything is reduced to the level of what it provides for a person, even having a nice home for example, it is important only to the extent that it provides positive experiences and minimizes the occurrence of negative experiences. Virtually anything in life, any event, any activity, and any possession, can ultimately be reduced to the kinds of experiences that they produce and it is these experiences that determines one's quality of life. In other words, when you "drill down" to the basis of any activity, event, or possession you own and ask why it is important or what it provides, you will eventually come to the level of experience. For example, if you buy a new car and you enjoy it, you can drill down to the level of experience and see that it ultimately provides you with experiences like comfort, prestige, freedom from worry about the car breaking down, a sense of accomplishment, or similar experiences. It is not the car itself you enjoy, but the experiences that it provides. What the three most basic positive and negative experiences are, how many of those you need, and in what proportion, positive to negative, is the subject of this book.

This book will describe a simple, yet powerful, method for you to assess your own QOL and specific techniques for you to improve it. You will be able to compare your score to the scores from hundreds of other people to see where you stand in terms of your QOL. Then we will examine each score and point out the most likely ways your QOL can be improved. Although the procedures are easy to follow, they require effort and commitment on your part. Everything that is worthwhile requires some effort to achieve it. If you put out the effort, you will be very pleased with the results. This book is designed to help you derive as many positive experiences from your life as you can. By reading this book and following the recommendations, you can expect to increase your QOL by 20% to 60% over a six-month to one year period.

Most of this book is devoted to teaching relatively simple techniques for accomplishing this goal. Additionally, this book contains many interesting and useful worksheets in the Appendices that will help you with this process. We will start immediately by having you take the Quality of Life Questionnaire. Actually, it's not really a questionnaire, it's only one question. Next, we will describe the ten principles in our theory of Quality of Life. Finally, we will describe both the general and specific steps you can take to improve it. In addition to describing ways to increase positive experiences in life, this book will also describe some of the latest and best techniques to reduce negative life experiences.

CHAPTER 2: WHO THIS BOOK IS FOR

This book is intended for three groups of people. The first is the general population, ranging in age from 18 to 95, who have an interest in improving their own quality of life. Our research has shown that age itself is no barrier to improving one's QOL. The second group for which this book is intended is people who are currently experiencing a low quality of life due to issues of being disadvantaged, being disabled, or suffering from any form of mental health disorder. Our research, and that of others, shows that these factors also are not a serious impediment to improving one's quality of life. Even people with terminal diagnoses can improve their quality of life for their remaining days through techniques described in this book. The third group for which this book is intended is therapists, psychologists, counselors, and physicians interested in better understanding the patients that they are working with and developing better techniques for assisting them. Often it seems that health interventions are described as being aimed at improving quality of life. However, there is often a lack of understanding about how an intervention (such as a new form of surgery) will truly help a person's quality of life. This book describes techniques to more directly affect quality of life outcomes.

Let me give you several examples of cases where the issue of quality of life was central to understanding the person. I know a 75-

year-old woman who had polio as a teenager which resulted in the paralysis of her entire body. Nevertheless, when asked about her level of QOL, she reported hers to be very high. When asked how she was able to maintain such a high QOL, it was evident that her productivity as a writer, her work with others, and her quest for understanding life on a spiritual basis contributed to her QOL. In other words, she had high amounts of positive experiences and relatively few negative experiences despite her disability. The only thing preventing her from having an even higher QOL was not being able to stay in a spiritual state longer. From this example, we can see that nearly everyone is capable of doing something they value, and everyone is capable of experiencing things that they find positive in life.

On the other hand, consider the following true case. A very successful farmer came to a clinic at the urging of his wife. He reported that he had lost his enthusiasm for farming and for much of his life. He said "I plant the corn, and the corn grows. I harvest the corn, and I start all over. What difference does it make? What does it all mean?" His QOL score was very low. This man was physically healthy, but was clinically depressed. He was obviously having far more negative experiences physically, psychologically, and interpersonally than positive experiences. His treatment was medication and psychotherapy for his depression. The psychotherapy, in good measure, was based upon principles in this book aimed at improving his quality of life. At the end of one year he reported "Isn't nature great? I planted this little seed and it grew into a marvelous plant. Imagine that! I'm not only helping people in this country but probably people in other countries as well. Boy, doesn't that feel good?" His final QOL was very high.

QUALITY OF LIFE

The level of writing in this book is aimed at people who have at least a high school level of reading ability. Many people with less than a high school level may also profit from reading this book. We have tried to make the concepts in this book as understandable as possible for the general population. Importantly, we have found that educational level has little bearing on one's quality of life. That is, in our research, which included people with educational levels from sixth grade to graduate school, there was little relationship between education level and level of quality of life. The significance of this finding is that you do not have to have a high educational level to have or to gain a high level of quality of life.

CHAPTER 3: DO YOU KNOW THESE PEOPLE?

On Wednesday, January 20th, 2010, a 13-year-old Haitian boy was interviewed on the television evening news. It was just a week since the devastating earthquake had flattened most of Haiti, killing thousands of people. It also destroyed this young boy's house, his father's workplace, and most of their belongings. The newscaster interviewing the boy noticed he had made several small toy cars out of some old bread dough, some lollipop sticks, and some caps from bottles of water which he used as wheels attached to the sticks. He made enough cars for himself and a few of his friends. After having attached a string to them they could race the cars. When the interviewer asked him why he did this when there was so much destruction around him, he said, "I want to improve my life." This young boy was somehow able to deal with the enormous destruction and his own personal distress well enough to actually try to have fun.

The last thing Jerome Johnson remembers was an explosion. He woke up in Walter Reed Hospital with the loss of one leg, three fingers on his right hand and eyesight in his right eye. Jerome was a soldier serving in the Middle East when he received his life-changing injuries. Before he joined the Army, he worked as a carpenter and enjoyed an active recreational life and social life. Now, during his rehabilitation phase, he is wondering how he will ever get the quality of life back that he used to have. Getting that back is one of the most important things to him now. These two examples show that quality of life issues are among the most important for people, even people undergoing devastating circumstances. The need to gain or to regain quality of life is vital to everyone.

If the examples above are too extreme for you to relate to, consider the following examples.

Joe is driving home from work on his usual one and a half hour commute, making his way slowly through dense traffic on the freeway. He is wondering how he ended up spending so much time on the freeway, so much time at work, and spending so little time on himself.

Rita took a job promotion last year partly because it came with a large increase in her salary. Now she finds that she is not really as happy as she was before the promotion. She doesn't like having to supervise other people, she misses the technical aspects of her previous position, and she is bored by so many meetings.

Mary is a very successful attorney with an income well above $300,000 per year. However, she is considering accepting a much lower position in a non-profit group because she thinks she would be happier.

Richard suffered a major heart attack two months ago. His doctors have told him he has to change his lifestyle, and at the same time Richard, at age 54, is reflecting on what life is all about.

Kathy is a married mother with three children. This is the role she always desired. However, for the last six months she has noticed that she has lost much of her enthusiasm and she rates her life as just so-so, neither good nor bad.

If any of these scenarios seem familiar to you, you may ask

yourself what they all have in common. The answer is: each of these individuals' quality of life has been seriously affected by their choices, and consequently, by the number of positive and negative experiences they have.

CHAPTER 4: ABOUT THE AUTHOR

Bryan Kemp received his Ph.D. in Lifespan Developmental Psychology from the University of Southern California in 1971. Since then his career has been divided between clinical practice, teaching and conducting research. Among his different academic appointments, he has been Professor of Psychiatry (Psychology) and Behavioral Sciences in the Keck School of Medicine at the University of Southern California. He has also been Research Professor of Gerontology at the same institution where he studied aging. He is currently a clinical professor of Neurology at USC. He first developed interest in quality of life issues when he noticed the wide variety of ways in which people adjusted to aging. Although most people were facing more or less the same circumstances, the way they experienced it and related to it was quite variable. This interest in quality of life continued throughout his career and was a part of research he directed for nearly 30 years under federal funding. Most of this research dealt with people who had a physical disability, such as a spinal cord injury. Clinically, Dr. Kemp has seen thousands of patients, and again the issue of quality of life, or the lack of it, was a common theme across all populations. He began to publish articles about quality of life in 1985 and has continued to do so, evolving his ideas, philosophy and principles continuously. He has given more than 100 lectures on the topic of Quality of Life to various audiences both domestically and internationally. For approximately the last five years Dr. Kemp has become progressively more disabled himself, having a neurological disorder that no one quite understands. He is currently almost completely paralyzed and almost completely blind due to this illness. However, he has continued his work on quality of life issues and incorporated his own recent experiences into some of his thinking. The bulk of his thinking and philosophy about the subject, though, goes back about 40 years, long before the onset of his disability. But there is no denying that knowledge of how to maintain a high quality of life has been a blessing for him. It has also made it possible for him to enjoy a rich family life, many friendships, and lots of interesting activities.

YOUR QOL

CHAPTER 5: QOL – WHERE ARE YOU?

Are you ready to get started? In Figure 5.1, you will find a simple scale containing 7 cells numbered 1 through 7. Please turn to Figure 5.1 now. In a moment, we will get to the directions. For now, notice that the scale ranges from "life is very distressing" to "life is so-so," neither good nor bad, to "life is great." In a moment, you will be asked to make a mark in one of these cells to describe where you are in terms of your QOL. Please record the date by your score so that you can recall when you took it. The main thing is to be honest about yourself. Do not try to impress others. Realize this is a tool for you to improve your QOL. If you cheat, you will only be cheating yourself.

Here are the instructions: Taking everything in your life into account, please rate your overall QOL using the following 7 point scale. One (1) means life is very distressing, it is hard to imagine how it could get much worse. Seven (7) means that life is great, it is hard to imagine how it could get much better. Four (4) means life is so-so, neither good nor bad.

Now, where are you? You may use a half point value if you want to; for example, 3.5 or 5.5. Place a mark on Figure 5.1 where it best describes your current overall QOL. If this has not been a typical week for you, for instance, if there has been a death in your family or you have been ill, or you have received a huge job promotion, etc., anything making this last week unusual, please wait for one month and then take this scale.

Figure 5.1

Quality of Life Scale

1	2	3	4	5	6	7

Life is
very
distressing   Life is
so-so   Life is
great

First, we can compare your score to the scores of approximately 1500 people who have taken the same scale in research studies. These people were sampled from many different locations in the United States. The people sampled were from various backgrounds, ethnicities, ages, and some with physical disabilities and others without physical disability. We cannot say that they represent a random sample of the United States population, but we believe they come close to it. The average score across all samples is 5.1. This represents the mean average. The most common score was 5; this is known as the mode. Whereas the middle of the scale itself is 4 (represented by the phrase "life is so-so, neither good nor bad") this was not found to be the middle or average score in our samples. The average score of 5 or 5.1 means that the average person rates their own quality of life as slightly positive. Approximately 15% of the sampled people scored below "4" on the scale. Approximately 20% obtained a score of "4". Approximately 28% scored a "5", 20% scored a "6" and 12% scored a "7". Our research has shown that there is very little relationship between QOL scores and age, income level, or physical disability. These results mean that people of any age, even all the way up to age 90, are capable of having a high QOL. Even people with severe physical disabilities are capable of having a high QOL. In fact, we found no difference between people with a physical disability and without a physical disability on the QOL measure. The reason for this is that people with physical disabilities can learn how to have as many positive experiences as their non-disabled counterparts, even if their disabilities are of different types.

Now, let's convert your score to a similar scale. The new scale can be found in Figure 5.2. It is very similar to Figure 5.1, except that different numbers are used in place of 1 through 7. The reason for converting your score to a slightly different scale is that the new scale makes it easier to understand low scores versus high scores versus neutral scores. That is, scores of 1-3 on the scale you just took are low and might be considered as a group to be "negative QOL". On the other hand, scores of 5-7 can be considered positive QOL scores. A score of 4, while below the mean, can be considered neutral because it is labeled as such on the original scale. We convert the scores on the original scale to scores on the converted scale to help make this distinction more clear. As you can see, in Figure 5.2 the middle score (4) on the original scale is now indicated by a 0 on the converted scale. Likewise, a 1 on the original scale becomes a -3 on the converted scale. A raw score of 2 on the original scale becomes a -2 on the converted scale. A score of 3 on the original scale becomes a -1 on the converted scale. As mentioned, the original 4 becomes a 0 or neutral. The 5 on the original scale becomes a +1 on the converted scale. A 6 becomes a +2 and a 7 on the original scale becomes a +3 on the converted scale. All you have to do is transfer your mark from Figure 5.1 to Figure 5.2 and put it in the same square.

Figure 5.2

Converted QOL Scale

Raw Scores	1	2	3	4	5	6	7
Converted Scores	-3	-2	-1	0	1	2	3
	Terrible	Very Bad	Bad	Neutral	Good	Very Good	Great

This conversion step helps to define more clearly the difference between negative QOL and positive QOL and it sets the stage for us to begin to discuss the factors that underlie each. Quality of life does not exist as just a positive entity. The daily experiences of life can also be distressing, painful, and upsetting and constitute a negative quality of life on a day to day basis. One of our goals is to help people move from a negative state of QOL to a more positive state as high as possible.

Next we will examine in more detail what each of these scores mean, and what you might expect in terms of improving your score over the next 6 to 12 months. In the next section, the theory of quality of life and the ten principles which underlie it will be discussed. This will give you additional help in improving your quality of life.

CHAPTER 6: WHAT DO YOUR SCORES MEAN?

We are now ready to begin discussing what each of the scores on the QOL scale mean. We will use the converted scores for this discussion; so if you haven't yet converted your score from the original scale to the converted scale, now would be a good time to do so. This section will give some general descriptions about each score based on our research and clinical experience. Specific steps and general strategies about what you could consider doing to improve or change your score will come in subsequent chapters.

A score of -3. If you scored a -3 on the converted scale, you are experiencing an abundance of distress in your life. This distress is either physical, psychological, interpersonal, or all three of them. You experience very few positive things in your life right now. Instead, your life has many unpleasant emotional feelings such as: depression, anxiety, dread, insecurity, sleeplessness, fatigue, and a lack of ability to cheer up, to enjoy things that you used to, or to enjoy things that others do. Physically, you may have a great deal of pain, difficulty functioning on a daily basis, or have serious health problems. Spiritually, you may have doubt about the meaning of life or your purpose and value. You probably have little hope that things can improve. Maintaining good relationships with other people, even though you love and care for them, is difficult right now. You may never have felt worse in your life. However, where there is great distress, there is also great hope for improvement. If you follow the recommendations in this book you can reasonably expect to move your QOL to at least +1 within a year.

A score of -2. Your score indicates that you are having trouble coping with some major issues in life, such as your health, your family, your job, or similar "big ticket" items, and you are not yet winning the struggle. However, you can overcome these things and have a better QOL. Right now you have a few positive experiences in life, but far more negative experiences. Try as you might, you have not been able to change the balance to have more positive experiences than negative experiences. There will always be some negative experiences. But you can't let them grow and dominate you and prevent you from having many more positive experiences than negative. The distress you feel is probably both emotional and physical, because those two are closely related. You can expect to be able to improve your QOL from its current point to approximately a +1 over the next 6 to 10 months if you follow the recommended steps in the following chapters. On a daily basis, in terms of how you experience your life, this will be an enormous change for you. It would be equivalent to living in Chicago during the winter versus living in San Francisco. San Francisco may not be your ideal city, but it certainly is a lot less stressful than Chicago in the winter.

A score of -1. If you scored -1, you join approximately 10% of the population who have the same score. While life is not terrible, it's not very fun or rewarding or meaningful. You are not far from being able to turn your life toward more positive everyday experiences rather than the frequent negative experiences you have now. A lot will depend upon how you learn to view things differently, how you cope with some underlying problems in your life, and how you begin to increase and fully experience positive things in your life. At this time, however, people around you may wonder why you appear so gloomy, unenthusiastic and unresponsive to their attempts to cheer you up. With effort and by following the recommended steps in the subsequent chapters you can reasonably expect to move to a QOL of +1 within 8 to10 months.

A score of 0. If you scored 0 (neutral), the best description for you is that life is so-so, neither good nor bad. You are truly in between. Research shows that you do not have overwhelming negative experiences, but you don't have many positive experiences either. The words "blah," "lost," and "lacking enthusiasm" come to mind. You may experience emotional states like uncertainty and ambivalence. You need a direction in which to move and the positive experiences that go along with that choice. We will see in the next chapter what kinds of experiences you are most lacking, and what it would take to increase your QOL. You can reasonably expect to move to a QOL of +1 or +2 within the next 6 to 10 months. Once you gain the proper perspective of where you are going, you will begin to reap the rewards.

A score of +1. If you scored +1, scores of this kind match the average across studies we have conducted. A +1 score means that your QOL can be described as "good" or "somewhat positive." You have more positive experiences in your life than negative experiences and that is what gives you your +1 score. You have realized that quality of life exists on the experiential level and you are seeking to have as many positive experiences as possible. You probably have a healthy way of coping with negative events. This allows you to minimize their impacts on your QOL. For the most part, you enjoy positive mental health and people probably enjoy spending time with you. You can, however, improve your QOL further. You can reasonably expect to improve to a score of +2 or possibly even +3 within the next 6 to 12 months by following the recommended steps in the next chapters.

A score of +2. If you scored +2, scores in this range are quite high. Your QOL can be described as "very good," "positive," or "very desirable." You clearly have an abundance of positive experiences of one kind or another in your everyday life. What others might see as a burden, you might perceive as an opportunity for doing good. The biggest differences between scores of +1 and +2 are that people who score +2 have been found to have a stronger sense of purpose or mission in life and they also are engaged in more activities that provide benefit to others, such as volunteering. You may wonder why you don't score a +3 on the QOL scale, but at the same time you have a pretty good idea what is holding you back from that last step. The recommendations in the next chapters will also help you attain that higher level of QOL.

A score of +3. Congratulations! Your QOL is great. Whatever you are doing, keep doing it. Most people who obtain this score share three characteristics. They are able to **experience** life fully, **express** it and to **share** it with others. At this level, you have inherent responsibility to share your secrets with others. It is time to spread the joy. You should seriously consider ways to disseminate your knowledge and your philosophy with others. Of course, this will also reinforce your own QOL and maybe add additional insights for you. You might think of going on-line, writing short articles, or speaking before groups, as a way of spreading the word to the world about your way of achieving such a high QOL. Undoubtedly, others would benefit a great deal. Maybe you should consider starting a +3 club.

This chapter has outlined what different scores on the QOL scale mean in general. In the next chapter, we will go into greater detail about what you can do to improve and/or maintain your QOL level. Your QOL is not fixed or permanent. It can be changed if you are feeling a need to restore it, or are willing to examine some of the underlying dynamics of QOL and are also willing to put forth some effort to improve it.

A THEORY OF QOL IN TEN PRINCIPLES

CHAPTER 7: A THEORY OF QOL

Prior to improving your own QOL, it will be helpful to understand some basic principles governing QOL in general. These principles are relatively simple and are supported by much previous research and practice. We will go through each principle, one at a time, and discuss the background of historical knowledge and recent research that supports it. You can also think of these principles as being a theory of QOL, wherein a theory is a set of principles that support each other through a combination of logic and empirical findings. This theory is easy to remember and may help you consider your own life, your priorities, and the lives of your family and friends.

The First Principle: Humans have an inherent desire to improve their lives.

As far back as evidence can take us, approximately 50,000 years ago, humankind has continuously been motivated to develop new tools, new techniques, and new technologies that benefit their well-being. From controlling fire, to inventing the Clovis point spear, to bow and arrow, to the wheel and eventually landing on the moon, humans have sought to shape their environment to their own benefit. It is not clear what the driving force is behind this expansionistic behavior. But it is clear that it exists. One simply has to look at the evolution of ideas, evolution of technology, and evolution of culture over the past thousands of years to see it in action. Most likely this continuous evolution of humankind is due to our ability to think and problem-solve and our motivation to reduce discomfort and increase well-being. In *The Ascent of Man*, Bronowski describes this exact process and further describes how new advances must await prior changes of technologies and cultures for the new technology to be accepted. For example, although Galileo was correct when he said that the sun was the center of the solar system, the church did not accept this belief. Public acceptance of this knowledge, and its subsequent applications, had to wait several centuries until the church acknowledged that the earth is not the center of the solar system. Further, anyone can notice the phenomenon of evolving technologies as they look back and recall what life was like in the United States in the 19th and 20th centuries. Changes in transportation, sources of energy, communications, education, basic technologies, increased life expectancy, and many other things have evolved significantly in just the last 100 years. This phenomenon will continue through and beyond the 21st century as long as humankind can think of new ideas and has motivation to carry them out. Moreover, the rate of advancement is accelerating, so it is often difficult for individuals to keep up with the pace of change.

The Second Principle: Improving *"conditions in life" can take two forms: improving one's objective situation or improving one's subjective quality of life.*

In Ancient Rome, there was a god for nearly everything. One of these was the god that governed the doorway to the house. Its name was Janus. You have probably seen the symbol of it. Janus has two faces, one is looking one way and the other is looking the opposite way. This represents its two dimensions. One face looked outward toward the objective world. It was looking for ways to improve or maintain objective conditions in life. The other face looked inward, into the house. This face represented securing and maintaining subjective qualities of home life, such as security, tenderness, warmth, and love. In a sense, this dual nature epitomizes the nature of human existence. We can look out from ourselves as well as into ourselves. The outward looking side of man is objective, and the inward looking side is subjective. Our outer self tries to control, improve, and maintain the objective factors in life that we believe will make us secure and successful. On the other hand, the inward looking or subjective view is how we experience life, whether we are happy or sad, distressed or elated, fulfilled or bored, successful or disappointed. Thus, we can divide conditions of life into two parts: objective (the outer view) and subjective (the inner view). This is the same as the difference between the physical world and the psychological world. In order to keep our thinking clear, we will call the objective condition of life the Standard of Living (LS), and we will call the subjective experience of our lives the Quality of Life (QOL). This is a common distinction made by many previous writers in philosophy, psychology, anthropology, or other human sciences. Today, measures of the objective conditions in life include such things as home ownership, income level, car ownership, level of education, etc. Subjective QOL, on the other hand, is measured by the person's own view of his or her life. The subjective viewpoint takes the position that individuals are the best judges of their own QOL. Today this is often measured by life satisfaction scales, assessment of happiness, or, in our case, the quality of one's life.

Research has pretty well established that there is only a low or weak relationship between objective standards of living and subjective quality of life. After satisfying one's basic needs for shelter, food, safety and comfort, there is little relationship between increases in one's objective standard of living and one's subjective experience of quality of life. This is a very critical point and accounts for much of today's unhappiness among people who have their basic needs satisfied. Many people falsely believe that they can improve their QOL (which is subjective) by improving their standard of living (which is objective). This simply can't be done and people who try, but find out it doesn't work, don't know what to do next. Mathematically, the relationship between objective factors in life and the level of quality of life is about .20 to .30, which means that only about five to ten percent of what we consider to be quality of life is made up of the objective conditions in our life.

To further clarify this point, it is obvious that a person can be high or low on either of these factors (standard of living or QOL). At the extremes we can see the four different examples of prototypes in Figure 7.1.

These are examples of people who have one of four possible combinations of standard of living and quality of life: high on both standard of living and QOL; low on both standard of living and QOL; high on standard of living but low on QOL; and high on QOL but low on standard of living. In Figure 7.1, the top left square represents people who have a lower standard of living, but still have a high quality of life. Mother Theresa is an extreme example because she lacked even some of the basic necessities of life but had a very meaningful life due to the work she was doing. People who do not own a house, do not have high incomes, or do not have even a car, can still have a very high quality of life. They can focus on the things described in this book that lead to a high subjective quality of life, even if their objective standard of living is low. You see examples of these people around you all the time. They may be working for minimum wage in a market or restaurant, but when you encounter them you can tell by their attitude and their smiles and their positive interactions that they still have a fairly high quality of life.

Figure 7.1

Standard of Living vs. Quality of Life

		Standard of Living	
		Low	*High*
Quality of Life (QOL)	*High*	"The Saint" (e.g. Mother Theresa)	"The Philanthropist" (e.g. Bill Gates)
	Low	"The Homeless" (e.g. John Smith)	"The Fallen Star" (e.g. a well-known golfer)

In the top right square you find what we would probably all desire. These people have a high objective standard of living and they also have a high subjective quality of life. Their quality of life is not high because they have a high standard of living, but rather these people have found a way to have both. The epitome of this combination may be exemplified by Bill Gates, one of the founders of Microsoft. He is among the richest people in the world and his subjective quality of life is high, by his own accounts, because of his work through his foundation, his marriage, and the many things in life that he enjoys. Could he have a high quality of life without all of his material possessions? Probably so. Moreover, his ability to have a high quality of life when he was younger may have contributed to his developing his illustrious career.

In the lower left square we find people who are low on both material possessions and quality of life. Their daily life is filled primarily with distressing experiences such as pain, sickness, loneliness, confusion, and hunger. They also lack basic housing, money, transportation, health care, or other people. The extreme example of this is homeless people living on skid row. Improving their quality of life would require also improving their standard of living so that they are at least not suffering. After that, their subjective quality of life may be improvable. However, there is a certain level of standard of living that is required so that life is not a constant battle for survival. I imagine there are a few people who could have a high quality of life with such impoverished conditions, but they would have to be truly exceptional people, such as Mother Theresa.

Finally, the bottom right square illustrates people who seem to have all that they could desire materially but have a low quality of life. Many movie stars, professional athletes, and famous executives fall into this square. A certain golfer with the wealth to buy whatever might be desired has recently been having a fairly low quality of life characterized by distressing physical pain, emotional pain, interpersonal problems, loss of prestige, and outbreaks of temper. Other actors and actresses are frequently in newspaper articles and magazine articles demonstrating their continued "falls from grace" that certainly appear to be representing lower levels of quality of life than would be expected.

Thus we can see that there is a clear distinction between the physical standard of living one has and the subjective, non-physical quality of life one possesses. This fact should give hope to anyone desiring to have a higher quality of life because, except in extreme cases, nearly anyone can increase their quality of life without necessarily improving their standard of living. Further, concentrating only on increasing your standard of living will not guarantee that you will have a high quality of life, increased happiness, or increased life satisfaction.

This book is about how to improve your QOL. It is not about how to improve your standard of living. However, you may find that your standard of living does improve some when you concentrate on improving your QOL.

The Third Principle: Increasing one's standard of living may or may not improve one's QOL.

There is only a moderate relationship between standard of living and QOL. Many researchers, including ourselves, have found the same result. If you picture QOL as a pie, approximately 25% of it is composed of the standard of living (LS) variable. As you have already read, the standard of living includes such items as levels of income, quality of housing, type of neighborhood, numbers of cars, educational level, etc. Advertisers and others would like you to think that the relationship between standard of living and quality of life is larger than it is. That way, they can sell you more products and promise that it will increase your quality of life, even though that argument is patently false. The other night, I was listening to an advertisement from a prestigious German auto maker who promised that if you bought their product, what comes along with the car is an experience of joy. In other words, they are promising to increase your QOL by raising your standard of living. What they neglect to mention are the experiences associated with the initial high price of the vehicle, the monthly payments and the expense of gasoline. Instead the automaker chooses to focus on the joy that you would experience from owning one of their cars. It also avoids saying that there are other ways of experiencing joy besides buying an expensive automobile. However, the automobile company is correct when it recognizes that people are looking for ways to increase their subjective quality of life. They were also right when they suggested that certain kinds of experiences underlie what we call quality of life. Most people have a need, and many have a hunger, for that mysterious thing that makes their life worth living on a daily basis. That thing turns out not to be a "thing" at all but certain psychological experiences that we all need in order to have a high quality of life. The difficulty for people so far has been trying to identify what experiences are necessary, how to obtain them, and what we actually mean by "experience". As this book unfolds it will reveal what an experience is and the kinds that make life worthwhile and of high quality.

More recently Craig Easterbrook has described this same phenomenon in his book, *The Progress Paradox*. The paradox he describes is this: even though the standard of living has increased for most people over the last 100 years, the average QOL apparently has not. Many people try to increase their own QOL but aren't exactly sure how to go about accomplishing it. Our mass media tell you it is through more and more consumption, but that is clearly not working. People are looking for improvements in their experience of life and finding that it is not something that can be bought. Consistent with this is that many people will rate their QOL to have been highest when they had fewer material possessions and a simpler life. This is referred to as "the good ol' days" phenomenon.

The Fourth Principle: QOL is bi-directional.

By the term "bi-directional", we mean that there is a negative side to QOL and a separate positive side to QOL. Quality of life doesn't exist only as a positive attribute. If this were true, then we would only have to measure how much of this positive attribute each person had. By this we mean that QOL does not exist on a scale where there is simply a little of it, more of it, and a lot of it. Instead, QOL ranges from negative to neutral and from neutral to positive. The absence of negative QOL does not mean a person has a positive QOL anymore than the absence of illness does not mean that the person is healthy, nor does the absence of poverty mean one is rich. Instead, there is a midpoint where one is neither. QOL progresses from negative to neutral and *then* from neutral to positive. Reduction in negative experiences constitutes an improvement in QOL. In other words a change in QOL from -2 to -1 is the same degree of improvement as from +1 to +2. Changes on either side, negative or positive, change the overall QOL.

Negative QOL is dominated by distressing experiences compared to relatively few positive experiences. On the other hand, a positive QOL is dominated by an abundance of positive experiences and relatively few negative experiences. A neutral QOL is characterized by having an equal number of positive and negative experiences. At this neutral point, a person may find themselves restless, drifting, unfocused, and mildly unhappy. This one dimensional, two-sided model of QOL was highly influenced by the work of Herzberg concerning job satisfaction in the automobile industries during the 1960's. He developed a one dimensional, two-sided model of job satisfaction similar to our model of QOL. He discovered that there were many conditions of work that made people dissatisfied. These included such things as hourly wage, benefits, working conditions, and lack of job security. However, when these conditions were improved, workers were not dissatisfied; but they were not satisfied either. Not being dissatisfied was not the same as being satisfied. In order to be satisfied, workers needed to have other conditions met. These included increased control over product quality, increased control over the production line, and an improved communication method between line workers, supervisors, and executives. Herzberg labeled the first set of variables as the **hygiene factor**, and he labeled the second set of variables as the **motivation factor**. His conceptual model made good sense for our research, so we incorporated it into our model.

The Fifth Principle: *The main ingredients involved in either negative or positive QOL are the experiences in your life.*

The first thing you are likely to ask yourself is, "What does 'experience' mean?" That's a very good question. I'll try to answer this using a more psychological perspective. The kind of experience I am talking about is not like a job resume where you can say you have 10 years of experience as an accountant. Instead, the experience I am referring to is an inner psychological experience in which both feelings and thoughts are involved. An experience is like a psychological version of a molecule. A physical molecule is a collection of several atoms all bound together. It may consist of a carbon atom, a hydrogen atom, an oxygen atom, and a nitrogen atom. We can draw a parallel psychological "molecule." In this case, the "experiential" molecule is also made up of four "atoms" which in their natural state are all bound together. These "atoms" are: 1) feeling/emotion, 2) thoughts/perception, 3) bodily reaction, and 4) behavior/action. Together these constitute an experience. For example, when you hear a joke for the first time and you find it funny, you may experience something like joy, or a thought like, "That was funny." Your body releases positive chemicals into the body and brain, and you laugh. You have experienced the joke. Perhaps you know people who don't really appreciate a joke, and they only say, "That was funny." They don't seem to have really experienced the joke because they leave most of the "atoms" out of their experience. For some reason they are blocked off from either experiencing or expressing the other components of the psychological molecule. Likewise, when people are sad and fully experience the sadness, they have the feeling of being sad, the relevant thoughts about what they have lost, the relevant physiological changes, and they act sad. People who are unable to experience sadness will have only a component or two of the experience. The person who can experience the sadness will resolve it much sooner than the person who can only experience part of it. People who are able to fully experience things are able to move from one experience to another experience more readily. The reason for this is once having had a full experience, it begins to dissipate.

Being able to fully experience events in life leads to more joy and excitement. For example, I was watching a friend watching a football game on TV the other day. His team made a great play and advanced the ball 40 yards. His reaction to this was to shout, "Hurray!" and to thrust his arms into the air as a gesture of enthusiasm, to say, "What a great play," and to conclude by saying, "I really liked that." You can see that he had a full experience in relation to what he was watching. It's no coincidence that he is also a successful psychiatrist and that he is able to accurately understand other people's experiences. If you want to see someone who is really able to experience things fully, just watch an infant who is beginning to crawl and explore his or her world. They are fascinated by simple things, such as a plastic cup or some paper that will crumple. If they are normal, they will show a full experience by their reaction to exploring these objects. They will giggle and laugh, they will make the cup and paper reproduce the sound over and over again. Clearly they are delighted, and even though we are not sure what they are thinking, we believe it's something positive. If infants are unhappy about something, they also experience and demonstrate it fully. They cry, scream, have tears, throw their arms around, and whine. However as soon as they get what they want, the unhappy experience ends and the happy experience starts again.

Everyone should strive to have the quality of experience that infants do. Let me give you a couple of examples of what I mean. Remember the last time you fell in love. Recall that you had certain thoughts, certain feelings, certain changes in your body, and certain behaviors. That "package" taken together was your experience of love. Next, remember the last time you were angry. Recall your thoughts, and recall your feelings, recall how it felt in your body, and finally recall your behavior. If you had a complete "package," we call that experience "anger." In either of these examples, if you didn't have one of the four elements or one of the elements was disproportional to the other ones, you didn't have the full experience. In a full and balanced experience, all four elements are present and they are mutually balanced. If you have a balanced experience, it yields an additional experience of feeling centered, in harmony, or in the moment. The book listed in the final chapter entitled *Zen and the Art of Motorcycle Maintenance* is an example of this. You can see the same phenomenon among great actors and great writers. What distinguishes a great actor or a great writer from an average one? Why is Meryl Streep always a superb actress and why was Hemingway such a great writer? The answer is that they could both capture the total experience of their characters either through acting or through written words. The more of the four elements of experience they can accurately capture, the more the audience feels that the artist has portrayed the real character. By the time Meryl Streep portrayed Julia Child in the movie "*Julie and Julia*," she had mastered all of the appropriate gestures, expressions, feelings, and thought processes. One could not tell the original from the actress.

Sometimes people have difficulty expressing one or more of these four elements and it becomes a problem. For example, a person who cannot express normal grief upon the death of a loved one, especially the feeling component, is at high risk for developing a depressive episode. A person who has a phobia expresses the fear but has no understanding of the conscious or unconscious thinking that leads to the fear. Some schools of thought in psychology or psychiatry focus on one of these four elements to the exclusion of the others. Thus, we have behaviorists who focus on a person's behavior, we have cognitive therapists who work on the thinking element, we have emotion based theories of developmental and abnormal psychology, and we have physiologically based theories, especially in psychiatry and neuropsychology, which focus on changes in the brain and elsewhere in the body. The approach in this book is holistic. That is, all four elements should be considered together. When a person truly has a positive experience, they will usually have the cognitive, emotional, behavioral, and physiological aspects of it. If they don't have all four components, they are restricting themselves, but there is usually no harm done. On the other hand, the same is not true of negative experiences. When some event occurs that is deleterious, traumatic, or injurious, it usually leads to negative subjective experiences. If these negative experiences are denied, or if only one or two elements of them are allowed to be experienced, then the other aspects of them may not go away. For example, we expect that, when a person dies, others – particularly those closest to the person – will show grief. Grief is a normal response to a loss. If, however, one only experiences the cognitive and the behavioral aspects of grief (they say they miss the other person and they begin to lead life without them) but they fail to show the emotional or physiological aspects of grief, these latter two components will not go away properly. Instead, unexpressed grief may become depression over the course of several months, or possibly a sleep disorder or eating disorder. However, if these components can all be experienced or expressed then they will dissipate in a normal fashion. The non-expression and non-experience of various components associated with negative events in life is a cause for many longstanding psychological problems. Encouraging the full expression of negative experiences helps in dissipating them.

Kinds of positive and negative experiences:

If you take a lifespan developmental approach to examining the kinds of positive experiences described in the literature, or if you examine the types of psychological themes common across cultures, it becomes evident that there is more than one kind of positive experience in life. Broadly conceived, there are three kinds of positive experiences that occur throughout a lifetime. The first one is **pleasurable** experience. By pleasurable we include many similar descriptors, such as joy, fun, excitement, novelty, sensuality and sexuality. Every culture, and indeed perhaps every species, is capable of experiencing some form of pleasure. Moreover, these experiences are typically displayed in a similar manner through smiling, laughing, repeating the behavior that causes the experience, and by feelings of enjoyment. You will notice that most pleasures come through the senses like vision, hearing and touch. The second form of positive experience relates to **success**. This includes terms such as achievement, accomplishment, competence, recognition, and advancement. As you will notice, the experience of achievement or success comes from how much control you can exercise over your environment and others. All cultures have symbols that allow their members to display their success, and success is often displayed through possessions or symbols. Thus simpler societies may display success by the number of cattle they own. Our society often displays success by the number of cars that are owned. Success and achievement are important in all cultures because they serve as motivators for improvement, both of the individual and of the culture as a whole. In our culture, a person is considered more successful if they own a home, but the country is considered more successful if everyone owns a home. The third form of positive experience relates to a **sense of purpose**, meaning fulfillment, higher understanding, values, spirituality, and having a mission. You will notice that these experiences are grounded in something larger than one's self but are more determined by one's self. Attaining an experience of meaning or purpose in life is important because it is not dependent upon possessions, but is determined rather by the value of the individual due to their knowledge, wisdom, or role in life. One may have high levels of enjoyment and accomplishment, but may lack a sense of purpose or meaning in life. This is often the case in overachieving or hedonistic individuals.

These three kinds of positive experiences emerge and become important at different points across the lifespan. In childhood "the pleasure principle" rules. This means that in infancy and beyond, having experiences of pleasure, enjoyment, and fun, brought about by touch, play, and interaction, are the strongest motivators in behavior. Children respond to playing "peek-a-boo" for long periods of time and can enjoy having their hair brushed for several minutes. Developmental psychology shows that children, from birth to about age 10 or 12, are primarily motivated by pleasure. They like to play, explore, seek novelty, be held, and experience new sensations and excitement. They are not very concerned about future matters such as making a living or the meaning of life. Having more pleasure in childhood, compared to the amount of physical or psychological pain, results in a well adjusted child, whereas the opposite is also true.

Children who experience an abundance of painful emotional and physical experiences have a great deal of trouble in life and their QOL also suffers. Sometimes an over-emphasis on pleasure as the only source of positive experience continues to be present as people become teenagers and adults. They don't seem to be fully-maturing teenagers or adults. So, for example, a teenager may be only interested in music, friends, playing video games, going surfing and eating. An adult may be retarded in their development by primarily being motivated by pleasure resulting from sports, sex, eating, or "hanging" with friends. Throughout life course the pleasure principle continues and is a principle form of gratification, motivation, and choice of behavior. However, other experiences should also become important. As a person begins to develop into an adult, experiences related to achievement, distinction, success, and advancement generally become equally important.

By the mid-teens people learn that they are expected to be able to contribute to their own economic and physical independence, and therefore need to become successful at something that leads to this. In the book *Little Women* by Louisa Mae Alcott, there is a section where the four March girls are all in their teens and they are putting together a theatrical play for their parents. They all agree that not only do they want it to be fun but they want it to be good enough so that they are successful at it. Here we see the transition from childhood to adulthood that we call the teenage years. Beginning in young adulthood, the achievement motive and the desire for economic advancement or recognition are behind the pursuit of activities that result in a sense of success. The experience of success or achievement cannot be underestimated because it is the primary motive for most of adult life for most people. Also, the achievement motive has led to the great economic success of the United States. We should not discount the value of the experience of achievement or success on the individual or on society. People in middle age often determine whether they are a success or a failure by how much they accomplish, what they produce or how much they earn. This need to achieve often brings with it a strong need to compete with each other, in both men and women. Although most men tend to deny it, they are highly competitive both at work and at leisure. This competitive nature is good in one sense, because talented people often succeed. However, it can be harmful if too much emphasis is placed on achievement and success as the only important outcomes in life.

Additionally, the focus on achievement and success means that one wants to display the signs and symbols of success: the largest homes, the newest cars, the best vacations and the best plastic surgery that money can buy. These image enhancers undoubtedly result in an objectively higher standard of living, but as we already know, the standard of living accounts for only a quarter of the quality of life. One of the drawbacks to being highly successful is that time becomes an obstacle since there is only so much of it in a day.

People who are very achievement-motivated and competitive go through life on a fast pace of multi-tasking in order to get more done. However, a high QOL requires you to go slow enough to be able to fully experience the positive aspects of life. Nevertheless it is quite normal and natural for people from roughly 20 to 60 to like and appreciate the experience of being successful, making advancement, being productive and making a difference.

Finally, by the time people reach late adulthood, sometimes

well before then, they find that they want more than simply fun and accomplishment. They also seek meaningful experiences in their lives, such as deeper understanding of the life cycle, the importance of philosophy, the need for charity, and the importance of having a purpose in life. Today, people hunger for that "something else" that makes life worth living and brings everything into perspective. This mysterious something appears to be a strong purpose, or a mission that makes life meaningful. The need for meaningful experiences may be met through religious activities, charitable activities, by sharing of one's wisdom, or through personal growth.

We know from research involving older individuals that without such experiences most develop a sense of emptiness or despair. Further, we know from other research findings that people who score high on a Purpose in Life inventory adjust better not only to late life but to the negative events that often accompany late life. Several years ago I had a patient who retired from his job at the university as a professor of theater arts. His position provided him with lots of pleasure, much admiration, multiple achievements and a high sense of success. Most of his life was tied to his identity in this role. Following a long-anticipated retirement, he developed some unusual symptoms, among which was an inability to resist writing down all of the license plate numbers of cars he passed on the freeway. This obsession and compulsion continued and expanded to include writing down lists of other things as well. The underlying problem was that these behaviors were masking a depressive disorder brought about by the loss of the pleasure of all the successful experiences he obtained through his work. When he had no way to replace them, he fell apart, had no meaningful activities in his life that could supplant what he no longer got from work, and his entire life disintegrated in front of him. His quality of life sank from a 6 before he retired to a 2 after he retired. He needed extensive treatment for his depression, but in order to get his quality of life back up to where it was, he needed to find ways to restore some of his successful experiences and, especially, to figure out what was now meaningful to him.

Figure 7.2

Percentage of Positive Experiences From Each Category Across Ages

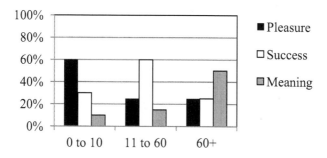

Thus, each of the three sources of positive experience play vital roles throughout the lifespan. Research findings suggest that people who have a blend of all three kinds of positive experiences (pleasure, success, meaning) have higher levels of QOL. The proportion of the blend changes with age so that in childhood, pleasure predominates and in late life, meaning plays a much larger role. A blended set of positive experiences is probably the most likely to provide a high quality of life. This is displayed in Figure 7.2. In it you will notice that in childhood the largest proportion of positive experiences is of the pleasurable kind, whereas people moving towards adulthood show the major proportion coming from successful experiences. In later life, the proportion coming from meaningful experiences is the largest. In a way, we lead our lives as if we were Calvin and Hobbs in childhood, Horatio Alger in midlife, and Abraham Lincoln in late life.

People vary in their need and desire for positive experiences. Which kinds of experiences are most important for them at a given time of their life, and what kinds of activities will lead to those experiences, also vary. Therefore we must make room for some wide allowances for individual differences. Most people derive their experiences from what they do or what type of activities they are involved in. The second important point is that there should always be a blend of these different experiences. Finally a point worth mentioning is that many people gain a strong sense of meaning and purpose earlier in their lives due to circumstances that are usually traumatic, such as the early onset of cancer, a severe disability, being personally traumatized or having a near death experience. To these people, issues concerning the meaning and purpose of life often emerge in response to their situation. Thus a 30 year old person returning from war with a traumatic injury may begin to examine issues regarding the meaning of life much sooner than they might have otherwise.

An additional point worth mentioning is that we need to distinguish between the experiences people have and the activities that help to promote them. We cannot assume that everyone derives the same experience from the same activity. We must find activities that promote positive experiences. For example, two people can be involved in the same activity, but derive completely different experiences from it. Everyone seeks the type of activities that bring them the most positive experiences of pleasure, success, and meaning. Activities generate those positive experiences, and we seek external activities because those activities give us the experiences we want. The more positive experiences a person has in their life compared to negative experiences, the higher their QOL.

Similarly, there are three major kinds of negative experiences. The first is physical, in which the person experiences a great deal of pain, fatigue, sickness, weakness, and dysfunction. The second is psychological, in which the person experiences a great deal of anxiety, depression, worry, lack of control, delusions, rage, or frustration. The third is interpersonal in which the person experiences a high amount of isolation, alienation, loneliness, conflict, rejection, or a lack of support. The more negative experiences the person has compared to the number of positive experiences they have, the lower their QOL will be. Unlike positive experiences, negative experiences may emerge at any time in life. Truly troubled people have a preponderance of negative experiences very early in life, and this may harm not only their present mental health, but their future mental health and quality of life as well. For example, children who receive physical, psychological, or interpersonal abuse suffer a terrible childhood, but even if those events cease, they may have an impact on the person's future development. For example, abused children may never learn to fully trust adults later in life and protect themselves by staying isolated and under-socialized. An important point to remember for the purposes of this book is that no one leads life without some negative experiences. What's important, though, is to minimize the number of negative experiences and maximize the number of positive experiences in order to have a happier, healthier, and more quality-filled life.

The Sixth Principle: *The relative balance between positive and negative experiences determines your overall QOL.*

Notice that this principle does not focus on what particular activities a person engages in. Instead it focuses on the experiences people derive from the activities in which they are engaged, from the events that occur to them, and from their own internal processes, most importantly their customary way of thinking about the events in their life. We will talk more about these three sources of our experiences because each of them is very important in their own right. In a recent study involving 103 graduate students, we examined the relationships among QOL based on the numbers of positive and negative experiences they had during the previous week. We analyzed the number of positive and negative experiences per week for each level of QOL from 1 through 7. People who scored lower (scores of 1 through 3) on QOL had an average of 22% positive experiences and approximately 78% negative experiences for the week. People who scored at level 4 on QOL had an average of 35% positive experiences and 65% negative experiences. Note that the middle score of 4 actually belongs to the low range of QOL because people reported more negative experiences than positive experiences. Those who scored higher on QOL (5 through 7) had 68% positive experiences and 32% negative experiences for the week. As you can plainly see in Figure 7.3, as the percentage of positive experiences increased and the percentage of negative experiences decreased the person's QOL was higher. Note that the shift in percentage of positive and negative experiences occurred between QOL of 4 and QOL of 5. Notice also

QUALITY OF LIFE

that we did not ask people what activities they were engaged in, but rather the number of positive and negative experiences they had. With proper cuing, such as that provided on the Positive Experiences Inventory and the Negative Experiences Inventory (discussed later), people were able to identify and count experiences they had during the week. This did not prove to be difficult once the definition of an experience was provided. Also, these results were highly reliable when we retested a subsample of the group a week apart.

Figure 7.3

The Relationship Between Positive and Negative Experiences and QOL

Level of QOL	1	2	3	4	5	6	7
Percent Positive	7	14	36	39	61	73	75
Percent Negative	93	86	64	61	39	27	25

Note further that the results are consistent with principle four, which stated that quality of life was bi-directional. In other words, the group with the higher QOL scores not only had fewer negative distressing experiences, but added a larger number of positive experiences. Being free of distressing experiences of a physical, psychological, or interpersonal nature does not guarantee a high quality of life. Instead a sufficient number of pleasurable, successful, and meaningful experiences must be present.

We have not concentrated on the activities or events that are associated with either negative or positive experiences for two important reasons. First, it is very difficult to determine what kind of experiences a person may have when involved in any particular activity. One person may experience dancing as a joyous, playful, fun activity, while another person may experience dancing as an embarrassing, difficult, and unfavorable activity. However, if you ask them their experiences, they will be able to tell you what they were. Secondly, a listing of all potential positive and negative activities and events would be endless, whereas it is relatively more concise and helpful to focus on the few but important experiences common across all people.

The Seventh Principle: *The right combination of increase in positive experiences and/or reduction of negative experiences will result in an increase in QOL.*

It follows from the previous principle that it should be possible to state with some degree of confidence how much change in positive and negative experiences it would take to improve a person's QOL by one unit on a 7-point scale, or on the converted scale. This is a vital piece of information, because we need to know this before we can develop a plan to consistently change these experiences. Thus far, our evidence indicates that an increase in positive experiences and/or a decrease in negative experiences that equals a 25% change from the current levels will result in a one unit improvement in QOL. However, this must be a consistent change that continues over time. Table 7.3 shows the percentage of positive and negative experiences for each level of QOL. As you can see, as one moves from the lowest level of QOL to the highest levels, the percentage of positive and negative experiences changes. The low end of the QOL scale, which also includes QOL of 4 (or a score of 0 on the converted scale), is dominated by a high percentage of negative experiences. That pattern changes as QOL increases. Or, looked at the other way, as positive experiences in life increase and negative experiences decrease, QOL improves. This is a general rule, but please note it does not work for extreme scores. Of course it also varies by the person's current level of QOL. For example, you might think that the best way to improve QOL would be to increase positive experiences by 12% and decrease negative experiences by 13%, thus totaling 25%. However, a person with a QOL score of 6 or +2 on the converted scale might not be able to reduce their negative experiences by 13% because their number of negative experiences is already so low. Instead, they should increase positive experiences the most and decrease a few negative experiences. On the other hand, a person who scores 1 on QOL desperately needs to reduce the number of negative experiences in their life initially, and then begin to add more positive experiences. In this case, we might be looking to decrease negative experiences by 20% and increase positive experiences by 5% during the first two weeks of intervention.

We also discovered that the least amount of change in QOL that is noticeable to an individual is one-half of a unit on the QOL scale. This is an important piece of information because it provides frequent positive reinforcement to the person trying to improve their QOL. In a study we conducted concerning the treatment of physical pain, we found that reduction of this distressing experience (pain) by 50% resulted in an improvement in QOL by one-half of a unit.

The methods required to reduce negative experiences are different than the methods used to increase positive experiences.

These methods will be presented in the forthcoming chapters.

The Eighth Principle: Maximizing QOL is enhanced by sharing your experiences with others.

      Thus far, when we have talked about experiencing either positive or negative things in our lives, we have limited it to being able to sense these experiences or to let them into our consciousness. For example, a person may become aware of heat in their stomach as they become angry. Becoming aware of these negative experiences is the first step in reducing them. However, we have not discussed what to do next. Likewise, we have not discussed what to do with positive experiences once we become aware of them. For example, what should we do about positive experiences we have in life, such as having a meaningful experience or the experience of joy? What else should we do with these experiences besides becoming aware of them?

      The next most important thing to do with either negative experiences (those associated with low quality of life) or positive experiences (those associated with high quality of life) is to be able to share them with someone else. Giving expression to our experiences helps to dissipate the negative experiences and helps to lengthen the positive experiences. If you know many people with a high quality of life, you probably notice that they are not silent about those experiences; in fact they are just the opposite. They express what they experience, often in great detail. They can tell you what they experience cognitively, emotionally, physically, and behaviorally. A person with high QOL may tell you about a backpacking trip they had, but more importantly, they will tell you the experiences they had during the trip, such as the smell of the morning air when they arose, the feel of the sun on their bodies, or the sight of the sun going down in the evening. They both have these experiences and share them with others. People with more negative experiences (and thus a lower QOL) can certainly share these experiences with others, but there are two vital ingredients they are missing that prevent the negative experiences from lessening. First, they share their experiences with people who are not capable of helping them. Second, they fail to gain insight into how they are contributing to their own negative experiences. We will say more about dealing with negative experiences in a later chapter.

As far as positive experiences go, sharing them with others is not limited to verbally expressing them. Positive experiences can also be shared by touch or other bodily exchanges, by writing about the experiences, or by expressions of art, including painting, sculpture, and dance. Many people find that art is a powerful way to express positive experiences. In fact, think of the great writers that you have read. Notice that what made them great was their ability to put their experiences into a written format that conveyed these experiences to others.

The Ninth Principle: *People with the highest level of QOL need to disseminate their experiences to others.*

This principle is important because it emphasizes one way that QOL can be improved on a wide basis. It has been my experience through 40 years of research and a similar number of years in clinical practice and 5 years as a person with a severe disability, that high QOL is not associated with any particular demographic or life circumstances variable. Instead, people who score at the highest level seem to have found ways to have and maintain the proper blend of positive experiences and have learned how to minimize or better process negative experiences in their lives. This is important information that needs to be shared with others so that others can benefit from these "experts." It is really the responsibility of people who score this high to use whatever avenues are best suited to them to disseminate this information. Perhaps it's through talking with others, perhaps it's through writing articles or books, or maybe it's through some new mass media method. Whatever it is, the secrets of having a very high quality of life should not be kept to oneself but should be shared with others.

The Tenth Principle: Regardless of circumstances, anyone's QOL can be improved.

Because QOL depends upon the nature and the number of experiences a person has, there is virtually no limit to who can benefit from the procedures and techniques described in this book for improving QOL. It really does not matter if the person is 90 years of age or 19 years of age, it doesn't matter if they come from a lower socioeconomic background or a higher one, it doesn't matter whether they have a disability or not, and it doesn't matter what their ethnic or racial background is. Everyone is capable of increasing the number of positive experiences they receive or reducing the number of negative experiences. The two primary differences between "disadvantaged" individuals versus their regular counterparts are in the number of negative experiences they may be faced with and in the number of activities or events they may be able to participate in to improve the number of their positive experiences. For example, a child with cerebral palsy may have significantly more negative experiences due to pain, discouragement, and rejection than his age-matched counterpart. These negative experiences need to be minimized, but at the same time there must be avenues for increasing positive experiences. Participation in social, recreational, or entertaining activities may be of limited accessibility also. Thus, improving quality of life is often more difficult, not because of the person's age or ethnicity, but because certain circumstances bring with them a higher number of negative experiences and a lower number of positive opportunities. Nevertheless, these negative experiences can be reduced in anyone and, likewise, it is possible to find activities and events which provide positive experiences, even if it takes more searching and perseverance to do so. When the disadvantaged person finds a sufficient number of pleasurable, successful, and meaningful experiences, whatever the activities or events that cause these, then there is a very good chance to attain a high quality of life. To prove this fact, we examined quality of life levels in approximately 850 people who had a moderate or severe disability. Approximately 33% of the sample had a high quality of life (a 6 or a 7). Moreover, the quality of life scores were not associated with the person's age or with the severity of their disability. The secret is to focus on the importance of the experiences in providing a high quality of life.

Likewise, other conditions in life, such as low income, ethnicity, and educational level, have little bearing on the ability to have high QOL. These variables may relate to the kinds of activities or events that bring positive experiences, but they are not barriers to someone having a high number of positive experiences. For example, there have been recent justifiable complaints about the high price of being able to take a family to a professional baseball game. The cost to take a family of four can be well over $100. This price puts it out of range for many people. However, there is an alternative available for a family to get as much pleasure from being there as if it were in person. A family could have a picnic in their own backyard, invite over some friends, put a television outside, have a barbecue, and turn it into a special night of baseball. It could become a regular family baseball night once a week. Plus, there would be no crowding and parking to deal with.

In summary, we have presented ten principles or axioms that we believe govern how quality of life can be viewed and conceptualized, how it comes about, and how it is maintained. By conceptualizing quality of life as bi-directional, we can account for the fact that some people do not appear to have a positive quality of life, but neither do they appear to have a negative quality of life. These people are in the middle of the transition from low to high. It also points to the fact that removing or eliminating a low quality of life does not by itself ensure that a high quality of life will occur. A high quality of life will occur only to the extent that people also add positive experiences to their lives. Reducing negative experiences, while at the same time increasing positive experiences, is the usual process that most people follow.

HOW WE GOT CONFUSED: THE DIFFERENCE BETWEEN STANDARD OF LIVING AND QUALITY OF LIFE

CHAPTER 8: THEY USED TO GO TOGETHER

To many people, the term quality of life is new. Most people have heard the similar term called standard of living and many people take these two terms to be synonymous. However they are quite different and require a bit more explanation for the reader to fully appreciate what this book is about. As you read earlier, standard of living refers to a measure of the objective characteristics and possessions one has in life. These include: level of income, employment status, home ownership, neighborhood safety, number of cars owned, quality of public schools, neighborhood recreation, access to public transportation, and other things similar to these. Measures of these, and perhaps a few others, are taken together to define and provide a standard of living used to compare large groups of people over time, or to compare different groups of people at the same time. For example, during the administration of President Eisenhower, he requested a study of the standard of living of Americans in 1950 compared to 1900. The study conducted showed that Americans had vastly improved during those 50 years in terms of the number of people who graduated from high school, the number of homes that were owned, the number of homes that had electricity, the number of cars people had, etc. Clearly, America's standard of living had improved. As time went by, though, people began to realize that just because the standard of living went up, people didn't seem to be much happier. Concerns were growing about the quality of American life, especially when issues like smog, crowded freeways, the threat of nuclear war, and high rates of divorce were considered. In about 1970, research began to investigate how people felt about their lives and how much quality they thought they had. More than standard of living measures, which assess objective things in life, quality measures are needed to measure the "subjective experience" of life. For example, you may have a job, which would be objectively true and point towards a higher standard of living, but you might be very unhappy with your job which points toward a very low quality of life. This is what separates the standard of living from the quality of living. Naturally, there is some degree of relationship between standard of living and quality of life. Contrary to public opinion, however, it is only a moderate degree of relationship between them. Evidence shows that many people with high standards of living have relatively low QOL. An excellent standard of living may not predict an excellent QOL, and we all know people who are well-off economically but nevertheless rate their QOL as low. Likewise, many of us know individuals who have a relatively low standard of living but rate their QOL as high. These people seem to have found a secret to extracting as much quality from their everyday life as possible. One striking example is a 70-year-old woman with cerebral palsy living in a nursing home. She has relatively few material comforts, needs 24 hour care, and is in frequent pain. Nevertheless, she reports her quality of life to be excellent (QOL is 6 out of 7) because she enjoys every minute that she is awake. She has a lot of fun interacting with the staff, listening to books on tape, and greatly enjoys visits with her family. Despite her objective circumstances, she values her interactions with others. She, like Victor Frankl, finds meaning in life in spite of objective conditions that seem dreadful to the rest of us. She has somehow discovered how to have an excellent QOL. How is she able to do this? As a licensed psychologist, I can assure you that she and people like her are not faking it, they are not in a state of denial, and they are not mentally disordered.

Several investigators have studied the relationships between objective standard of living and subjective assessments of QOL. These include Angus Campbell and Joseph Flanagan. Each of them studied very large samples of people and measured the relationships found between standard of living and QOL. Campbell found that they had between 25% and 30% in common. In other words, about 25% of QOL is composed of standard of living factors. Flanagan found approximately the same thing. Then what accounts for the other 75% of QOL? This finding also means that a person with a high standard of living can have either high QOL or low QOL. Likewise, a person with a low standard of living can have either a low QOL or high QOL.

More recently in The Progress Paradox, Easterbrook described a similar dilemma. Over the last two or three centuries, the standard of living has improved. We have progressed with more and better technologies, more education, and higher levels of income. However, QOL stopped increasing somewhere around 1960 and since then the standard of living and QOL have been on different tracks. If we take a measure of standard of living and add to it a measure of health status, both of illness and functional ability, these combined scores would give us a reasonably good measure of a person's objective circumstances in their life. The same can be said about the relationship between life circumstances and perceived quality of life as was said about the relationship between standard of living and quality of life. That is, there is only about a 30% relationship between the two. In order to understand the relationship between standard of living and QOL a little better, we must look back historically (See Table 8.1). At one time, increases in standard of living or life circumstances led directly to improvement in perceived quality of life and there was a 1:1 relationship between these two.

For approximately 10,000 years, improvements in standard of living and QOL went hand in hand; that is, whatever improved standard of living also improved QOL. The improvements in QOL were due, in many ways, to the same things that led to an increase in standard of living; namely, improvements in technology. Consider the invention of the bow and arrow (which occurred about 10,000 BCE). This was a major advancement in technology. Before that invention, hunters had to get very close to their prey in order to kill it. This put them in great danger of being killed themselves. Armed with bows and arrows, hunters could be far away from their prey and still kill it. Long distance hunting increased their standard of living because it supplied more meats and preserved more people. It also decreased the physical dangers of close-up hunting. Improved hunting technology also provided more animal skins for clothing and housing. This new level of technology increased the standard of living which, in turn, appears to have directly improved QOL because it reduced many negative experiences (like being wounded by an animal) and increased many positive experiences (such as providing food and warmth).

Consider another advancement in technology: the cultivation of wheat and its cousins barley and rye. Prior to this advancement, people gathered wild wheat. Then they learned how to cultivate and how to make hybrid varieties of wheat. Thereafter, they could begin to control food production and particularly to be able to grow it where they wanted to. There was less hunger and starvation as food production was controlled and supplies increased. Reducing hunger and starvation improved the standard of living and again directly improved QOL since people had fewer negative experiences (hunger) and more positive experiences (feeling that they could control the source of their food).

The wheel was invented in approximately 3000 BCE. This technological miracle raised the standard of living for nearly everyone because it was a major way of reducing labor demands. Heavy items could be rolled on wheels rather than dragged along the ground. Eventually, goods and people were able to ride on carriages supported by wheels. In addition to increasing the standard of living for large populations, the wheel also directly improved the QOL of individuals using it. Once again, changes in people's objective situations directly improved their subjective experience of life. There was less fatigue, fewer injuries, and easier ways for people to exchange goods and products. This helped bring many diverse people together at a social level, which, in turn, could provide better social networks and better mutual understanding of each other. In those days the relationship between standard of living and QOL had been assessed at approximately 80%, compared to the 25% relationship found today. People learned (consciously or unconsciously) that improvements in their standard of living resulted in improvements in their feelings about their quality of life. The driving force behind improvements in standard of living then was the same as it is today: newer technologies. Thus, the order of events was advancements in technology, followed by advancements in standard of living, followed by improvements in quality of life. The improvement in quality of life was due to both reducing distressing experiences and increasing positive experiences. In essence, though, people learned that these three processes went hand in hand. This pattern of advancement continued for approximately 4,000 years, but was broken in the mid-17th century with the beginning of the Industrial Revolution, and culminated in the year 1960, according to Easterbrook. Advances in a person's quality of life could no longer be linked to further advances in technology and standard of living.

After 1960, there was a growing interest in the individual's quality of life and research began to focus on such subjective issues as what causes satisfaction, happiness, fulfillment, and contentment. You might say that interest shifted from the quality of life of a whole country (best measured by an objective standard of living index) to the individual's own quality of life. Here we discovered many of the factors that contribute to these subjective states of being.

In the middle of the 20th century, the standard of living in the United States and other developed countries was fairly high and going up. New technologies were being developed at an ever increasing pace. However, it was also about this time that investigators, government officials and industry leaders realized that the quality of life of individuals was not going up as much as the standard of living. In fact, since about 1960, quality of life measures have more or less remained stable while advances in technology and improvements in the standard of living have increased dramatically. People have become disillusioned, disappointed or confused about why changes in standard of living or conditions in life have not resulted in improvements in their experienced quality of life. Divorce rates are higher than ever, many people are disillusioned by organized religion, people still complain about not getting enough out of life, and mental health problems are more common than ever. Obviously, there is now only a partial connection between standard of living and quality of life. The position taken in this book is that this partial connection has always been true but was hidden from view because people are more likely to focus on objective reality than subjective experiences as long as they have unmet needs. We've now probably reached the point in history where improvements in QOL will rely more on the person's ability to have and create and manage experiences on a subjective level. People will need to generate and appreciate not only the objective things in their life, but pay equal attention to the subjective experiences of their life.

Figure 8.1

Standard of Living and QOL Throughout History

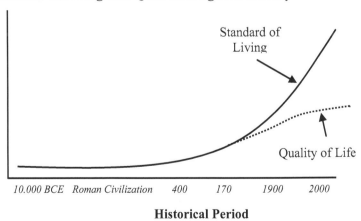

Historical Period

In summary, our quest has always been to improve our QOL. However, we have been operating under false assumptions. The first false assumption is that increases in standard of living will lead to increases in QOL. Therefore, the more things we have that make up the elements of standard of living (such as going to the right college, having a high income, living in the best neighborhood) will lead to a higher QOL. Secondly, we falsely assume that increases in technology will lead to increases in standard of living. We are, therefore, willing to pay money for the newest and best technology because we believe it will improve our standard of living which will in turn improve our quality of life. Lastly, we have falsely believed that we can purchase happiness or QOL. Instead, QOL is something you derive or create experientially from your various activities, encounters, and abilities.

CHAPTER 9: THE ROLE OF POVERTY, ILLNESS, AND DISABILITY ON QOL

Figure 9.1

Quality of Life and Standard of Living

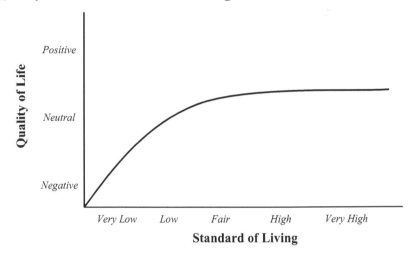

Your Life Circumstances and QOL

Up until this point in the story, we have more or less discussed the ideas of standard of living and quality of life as applied to the average person. But what about people who have disadvantaged circumstances due to poverty, illness, or disability? Can they hope to attain high or even average quality of life as compared to their peers, or do these difficult circumstances of life prohibit people from having as high a quality of life as others? The short answer to this question is that conditions such as these can have, but do not necessarily have, a major negative impact on QOL. In other words, anyone can have a high quality of life.

Disability

The role of disability in QOL is important enough that a separate chapter has been devoted to it later in this book. While at any given time approximately 13% of the population has a moderate to severe disability, over the lifespan approximately 55% of people will have a moderate to severe disability of one kind or another before they die. In other words, the majority of people will need to learn how to maintain as high a level of QOL as possible given the presence of a disability. The disability could be caused by a variety of illnesses and injuries - including stroke, Parkinson's disease, arthritis, heart disease, Alzheimer's disease, cancer, or such injuries as spinal cord severance, amputation, and loss of vision or hearing. It is, therefore, a very relevant topic for this book. From my experience both with and without a disability, the biggest problems in maintaining QOL are on both the positive and negative sides of the equation. Managing the many distressing physical, psychological and interpersonal issues associated with a disability without becoming a complainer, a nag, or a pain is vital to start with. A person with a disability probably has about three times as many negative experiences of one form or another on a regular basis, compared to a person without a disability. A disability is accompanied by psychological, physical, and interpersonal problems that, if left unaddressed, will result in a very low or even negative quality of life. It is well known, for example, that rates of depression among people with a disability are approximately five times as great as in the nondisabled population. This is evidence that some people cannot advance beyond a negative quality of life status, let alone develop a positive quality of life. However, if a person can deal with the most common negative experiences (see subsequent chapters for methods to do so), then having a positive quality of life is possible but as yet not guaranteed. Next, positive experiences must be discovered, developed, or modified to promote a positive quality of life. If they can deal with the negative experiences, then most people with disabilities can achieve a high quality of life if they can find alternative ways to satisfy their needs for sufficient pleasurable, successful, and meaningful experiences. More will be said of this in a later chapter.

Wounded Warriors

Armed Forces personnel who are injured in war or war-related activities represent a unique group where quality of life issues are especially important. Most wounded warriors will have sustained acute injuries to their bodies because the injuries are caused by explosions, bullets, shrapnel, collapsing buildings and crashes. These men and women sustain life-changing injuries in an instant. These injuries usually result in loss of vision, hearing, limbs or nerves that allow our bodies to work. Moreover, there are tremendous psychological "injuries" which occur. The most notable of these are depression, anxiety, and post-traumatic stress disorders. In addition to these clinical psychological conditions, there are numerous other psychological issues to deal with such as an altered self-image, concern over the acceptance of others, the management of pain, and the disruption of one's expected life trajectory. Evidence indicating the high rates of these problems has been published in numerous places. For example, suicide rates among active military or post-service personnel are approximately three times as high compared to the rest of the population. Post-traumatic stress disorders (PTSD) may affect as many as 20% of service personnel, with half of it being of the severe variety. Returning these dedicated personnel to a reasonable standard of living and a high as possible quality of life is a necessary and decidedly worthy task. In terms of quality of life, it would reasonably be expected that many, if not most, of these service people would need to find some altered ways of providing the necessary pleasurable, successful and meaningful experiences in life that give it a high quality. However, these facts also point to the likely notion that before we can talk about ways of increasing the positive experiences in life, we must help them deal with the overwhelming negative experiences they are having. That is, we have to give paramount importance to reducing the number of distressing experiences these people have. But again, the absence of distressing experiences does not guarantee the presence of positive experiences. It only allows for the possibility of positive experiences. Therefore, strategic interventions to help these dedicated individuals must focus on both sides of the quality of life continuum. We cannot be content with medical, psychological and rehabilitation efforts that only reduce the distress. We must also have programs that replace or enhance the kind and number of positive experiences that will allow these individuals to have as high a level of quality of life as possible.

Poverty

Poverty itself is associated with many negative experiences. These include multiple psychological stresses such as worry about meeting basic needs, crime in the community, and the high likelihood of encountering people with major mental health problems on a daily basis. Once again, the issue in gaining a higher QOL is finding ways to reduce these everyday negative experiences while trying to increase positive experiences. Poverty by itself does not cause a low quality of life.

Childhood and Adult Trauma

Unfortunately, many children and adults go through traumatic events that leave them with both physical and psychological scars for a long time. For a child, these traumas may include physical abuse, sexual abuse, abandonment, injury or neglect. For an adult, it may include traumatic injuries, multiple losses, or war time events. Often these events in childhood or adulthood come to interfere with or even dominate the person's life, making it difficult to have a high quality of life. Traumatic experiences from earlier in life often leave the person mistrustful of others, hyper-vigilant, anxious or depressed given these negative experiences. It is difficult to generate enough positive experiences to overcome these negative experiences in order to reach a very high QOL. In my experience, people with these traumas need both mental health treatment to help deal with the scars left by negative experiences, and some kind of life "coach" to help them generate a sufficient number of positive experiences. The traumatic event may never be undone, and the reaction to it may never be completely resolved, but people can learn to live with these residues better and learn how to make them interfere as little as possible in the quest for having a reasonably high QOL.

GENERAL PRINCIPLES FOR INCREASING POSITIVE QOL

CHAPTER 10: POSITIVE AND NEGATIVE EXPERIENCES

This chapter and the next one provide recommendations and instructions for improving your QOL. In these two chapters the primary focus is on steps you can follow to improve the positive aspects of your QOL. A separate section is devoted primarily to helping you better manage the negative aspects of your QOL. We will give you specific recommendations based on the converted score on the QOL scale. As you will recall, this converted scale changed the 1 to 7 range of possible scores to -3 to +3 with a 0 or neutral point in the middle. The reason we are using the converted scores on the QOL scale is to help you visualize how the balance between negative and positive experiences determines your overall QOL. For example, if your converted score is -2, you can easily see that you need to have far fewer negative experiences and more positive experiences to improve your QOL. The steps recommended in these chapters are designed to move you from whatever level of QOL you have to the higher levels, step by step. That is, it is difficult to help you have the highest level of QOL until we proceed through the other levels first. You can expect that it takes approximately 2 or 3 months to improve your QOL score one level on a consistent and well-established basis. It would not be reasonable to expect that you can improve your QOL dramatically in a short period of time because you need to establish and practice a new set of behaviors and viewpoints from one level to the next. Many people who believe that they can change their lives dramatically in a short period of time end up frustrated and defeated because they expected too much in the beginning. Like a ladder that you use to scale heights, you need to proceed one rung at a time in order to securely and reliably advance. People who try to climb a ladder quickly by skipping rungs often slip and fall back to where they started.

The main principle governing whether one has a positive QOL or a negative QOL is the number of positive and negative **experiences** they have on an everyday basis. People who have a negative QOL have a preponderance of negative experiences compared to the meager number of positive experiences they have each day and week. People with the lowest QOL may have so many negative experiences that they may wonder whether life is worth living. On the other hand, people who have a positive QOL have a higher number of positive experiences on a daily, weekly, and monthly basis compared to the number of negative experiences they have. It is impossible to escape all negative experiences in life, but the balance of positive experiences to negative experiences on a consistent basis is our goal. As you will recall, there are different types of positive and negative experiences. You can increase your positive experiences in a number of ways and, likewise, your negative experiences may be of one or more types. Learning how to increase your positive experiences in a variety of ways will certainly improve your QOL. Likewise, it is important to determine the primary source of negative experiences in order to reduce them as much as possible.

Notice that the emphasis is on the number of positive and negative **experiences** and not on the number and kind of activities in which people engage. This distinction is very important to understand. It is the subjective experiences people derive from their activities, events in their lives, and their own "self-talk" that determines their overall QOL. This emphasis on experience continues throughout this book. People who have the highest QOL scores emphasize their experiences in life as the basis for their scores. For example, people with the highest QOLs will report the way they felt and the experiences they had at a party more than the activity of attending the party itself. On the contrary, people with the lowest QOLs have not learned to focus on their inner experiences as the basis of their QOL, but rather report that it is the events and activities in their lives that cause their low QOL. In other words, people with higher QOLs have more of an "inner" focus compared to the "outer" focus of people with lower QOLs. There will be a further discussion of experiences in Chapter 11.

Now that you have learned the distinction between activities and experiences, we are going to get you to do a self assessment of the number of positive experiences you typically have. In order for you to think about the kind of activities that may give rise to positive experiences in your last week, you could examine the different schedules of pleasurable, successful, and meaningful activities that many people report have resulted in their positive experiences. These are in Appendices C, D, and E. However, be sure to remember that it is the number of experiences we want you to record, and not the number of activities. You may have more than one positive experience for a given activity, such as if you went to a party and enjoyed the music but also enjoyed how it brought you and your spouse closer together for the evening.

The first step to take in improving your QOL is to take the Positive Experiences Inventory that you can find in Appendix A. Regardless of your current level of QOL, this inventory will be very useful as we advance through the different levels of QOL. As we discussed in the earlier chapters, three different kinds of positive experiences are most important. These positive experiences include 1) pleasurable or enjoyable experiences, 2) successful or productive experiences, and 3) meaningful or purposeful experiences. The inventory you are being asked to take covers these various kinds of experiences. We are not interested in what caused these experiences, but only in the number of these different kinds of experiences you have. Please go ahead now and take the Positive Experiences Inventory that is in the Appendix A. Be sure to read the instructions before you begin and please remember to date it. After you have taken it, add up the total number of positive experiences you reported for the week.

You've done a good job so far! Now turn your attention to the Negative Experiences Inventory that can be found in Appendix B. Fill out this inventory the same way you did the Positive Experiences Inventory.

Using Positive and Negative Experiences Inventories

We now have two essential pieces of information that will help you in improving your QOL. We want you to continue to take these two inventories to help measure your progress and we suggest that you do so every two months. Be sure to date each form when you take it. Add up the scores on the Positive Experiences Inventory. Then do the same thing for the Negative Experiences Inventory, and find the total score for each inventory.

Next, examine the scores of the Positive Experiences Inventory. Look at the total number of pleasurable, successful, and meaningful experiences. Now do the same for negative experience scores. The most obvious thing to do is to compare the total number of positive experiences to the total number of negative experiences. Which is greater, and by how much? Our research shows that the average number of positive experiences per week across all levels of QOL is 16. If you scored a negative to neutral QOL, you will probably find that you have fewer positive experiences than average. Likewise, the average number of negative experiences per week across all levels of QOL is 12. If you scored a 0 or negative score on the QOL scale, you probably have more negative experiences than this. However, the most important thing is the ratio of your positive to negative experiences. A good way to do this is to determine the percentage of positive and negative experiences you have. To do this, add the total of the positive and negative experiences together. Then, to determine the percent of positive experiences, divide the number of positive experiences by the total number of experiences. Multiply the answer by 100. To determine the percent of negative experiences, subtract the percent of positive experiences from 100%. Now, in addition to seeing the sheer number of positive and negative experiences, you can also see the percent of each that you report in your life. By various strategies, we will help you reduce the number of negative experiences, increase the number of positive experiences, and increase the overall percentage of positive experiences you have compared to the percentage of negative experiences. Accomplishing these three things will be the basis for improving your overall quality of life.

Now let's look at the absolute number of positive experiences you indicated. First, look at what positive experiences you rate as the most important to you - those involving pleasure, success, or meaningfulness. Is the category getting sufficient time in proportion to its importance to you? If not, why doesn't it? This should give you an additional clue as to which type of positive experience might improve your QOL the most. The next thing you can do with the Positive Experiences Inventory is to determine what kind of blend of experiences you have. Do you have some of your positive experiences coming from each category? Or are most of your positive experiences coming from one category? Having a reasonable blend is important. The reason that a blend of positive experiences is important is that it provides a wider array of important experiences. Enjoyable and pleasurable experiences are the easiest to attain and they are the simplest kind. However, when they are not available, having other sources of positive experience is vital. When both pleasurable and successful experiences are minimal or not available, then meaningful experiences are still available and can provide a rich source of quality for a person. For example, soldiers at war may find their daily lives to have few sources of pleasure or success, but believing that their activities are for the greater good or are otherwise purposeful can provide enough positive experiences to overcome the many negative experiences of war.

A similar process holds true for the Negative Experiences Inventory. Hopefully, you have more positive experiences than negative ones. However, if the reverse is true, and you have more negative experiences than positive ones, and the percentage of negative ones is high, you'll know where you need to address your attention. Your overall strategy is going to be to reduce the negative and increase the positive experiences in your life. In other words, up with the good and down with the bad. What you have to do exactly will depend upon how extreme your scores are. Overall, it is a good idea to try to do both at the same time; that is, reduce the bad while increasing the good in order to make a bigger difference in the percentage of each kind of experience. For example, if you suffer from headaches and don't get out very much, do something about the headache and start to get out more at the same time. Stop waiting for your headaches to go away. **Any combination of consistent increases in positive experiences and/or decreases in negative experiences that totals 25% or more will increase QOL by one level.** We will discuss this more in the next section when we talk about specific steps you can follow.

Some secondary comparisons between the Positive and Negative Experience Inventories are also worth noting. Look at your positive experience score for pleasurable experiences. Now, compare that to the total of your negative experiences for the physical and psychological categories. Subtract one score from the other, and this will give you a rough idea of the amount of pleasure you have in your life compared to your physical and psychological pain. Ideally, the pleasurable experiences in your life should exceed the painful ones. If the reverse is true, then you see one area in which to begin your quest for improving your QOL. Of the three kinds of positive experiences - pleasure, success and meaning - increasing pleasurable experiences is the easiest way to begin. We will provide additional guidance for how to do this in the next chapter when we examine individual scores.

However, it is well known that people who are in distress do not engage in enough pleasurable and fun activities to counterbalance the painful experiences in their life. Although the effort to do this may seem immense, it is a necessary step in improving one's life.

Next, look at your score for success (achievement, accomplishment, etc.) and compare it to your score for negative social experiences. This comparison will give you a rough idea of the balance between your feelings of success, feelings of failure, and feelings of disappointment. The reason for this comparison is that success always involves feedback from other individuals telling you how they think you are doing. If your negative social experiences exceed your positive successful experiences, it will probably be difficult to attain or maintain a sense of success, or a sense of moving forward in life and accomplishing your goals. How can a busy housewife and mother feel she is a success if no one provides her with positive feedback and she is instead constantly unappreciated or undervalued?

Meaningful experiences are the only ones of the three types that encompass something larger than yourself. If you have a strong spiritual belief, a strong sense of purpose in life, a very important role in life, or have a sense of fulfillment, then the other kinds of positive experiences (and possibly negative experiences) don't have as great an impact on you. If you want to test this notion, use your imagination and follow the next situation mentally. Imagine there are two 40 story buildings that are 100 yards apart. A rope is suspended between these buildings at the 35th floor of each building. It is a strong secure rope, but the wind is blowing and it's cold outside. Your task is to crawl across the rope using your hands and legs. What would it take to entice you to crawl across, between the buildings, thus risking your life? Suppose someone offers you $10,000. Would you do it? No? Suppose someone offers you a large job promotion and lots of recognition for crossing this rope. Would you do it? No? Okay, now what *would* you do it for? Whatever you choose is going to be something that is meaningful for you. The answer might be something like: you would do it for God, or you would do it to save your child from falling out of a window, or you would do it to save your family from fire, or you would do it to save your country from an attack, or something else that is meaningful for you. This is what we mean when we say that meaningful activities are ones that encompass something larger or are more important than just yourself.

At the heart of QOL is the nature and number of experiences a person has in life. The secret to improving one's QOL is to increase the number of positive experiences, and to decrease the number of negative experiences to as few as possible. The person who experiences life to the fullest and the best, finds positive experiences in virtually everything. They eventually even learn how to turn seemingly negative experiences into positive ones. These people are said to be living in a state of bliss. When all of their experiences turn into meaningful, spiritual experiences, they are said to be living in a state of enlightenment.

To summarize this chapter, a general principle for improving quality of life is to increase the number of positive experiences in your life while decreasing the number of negative experiences. Two inventories were introduced to you to allow you to keep track of these experiences. You will find that if you follow this general principle, your QOL will slowly increase. Specific steps for doing so depend upon your current level of QOL and these will be discussed in the next section. Now we will turn our attention briefly to the question of why experience counts so much.

CHAPTER 11: THE SUPREMACY OF EXPERIENCE

Experience vs. Activity

Notice that throughout this book and in the Positive and Negative Experiences Inventories, we did not use the term "activity," such as positive and negative activities or positive and negative events. Rather we have used the term "experience". There are three important reasons for this distinction. First, QOL is a psychological term, and when measured from the individual point of view, the factors that go into determining QOL exist at the basic level in psychological terms also. The most basic psychological unit is experience. In fact, psychology emerged from natural philosophy when philosophers recognized that they could not discover the truth about "what is" until they could account for how the person experiences the world. Hence, the first psychological laboratory developed by Wilhelm Wundt in the 1890's was devoted to separating physical stimuli from the psychological experiences that went with them. The same is true today; the basic building block of consciousness is experience. Second, the relationship between different activities and different experiences is not direct. Two different people can derive entirely different experiences from the same activity or event. One person may like ice-skating and one person may hate it. One person may like opera while another finds it boring. We could never create a catalog of activities that everyone would agree produces a certain kind of experience. It makes much more sense to ask an individual what kind of activities bring them pleasure, success, and/or meaning, and to encourage them to engage in those or similar kinds of activities. Third, research shows that there is a stronger relationship between various kinds of measured **experiences** and QOL than there is between different kinds of **activities** and QOL. For example, several studies have shown that social participation (activity) correlates with QOL moderately. However our studies showed that a person's experiences of pleasure, success, and meaning correlated much higher with the same measure of QOL. Thus, it is not the objective activity that counts the most but rather the subjective experience the person derives from it.

You, as a reader, can also use this knowledge as a tool to increasing your QOL. That is, examine your own activities or events you encounter. What kinds of experiences do you derive from them? What activities do you prefer the most? What events bring you the most pleasure, success, or meaning? You will probably find that there are some that don't provide you with even a few positive experiences, such as housekeeping, shopping, doing dishes, etc. But there would be others you engage in that do provide you with some form of positive experiences: pleasurable, successful, or meaningful. You may have to focus inward for a couple of minutes to identify these experiences. However, if you have an activity that provides you with any of these positive experiences, then find other activities which also provide you with similar experiences and increase those.

Better yet, for each activity you elect to engage in or for each event you choose to attend (not those that you have to do) try to

identify the experience you are trying to create or have. Is it the experience of pleasure? Is it related to the experience of success or achievement? Is it related to the experience of meaning or purpose? If you are going to lead a life that is full and a life of high quality, it is extremely important that it be driven by the kind of experiences you want to have in life. The same is true for negative experiences. There are activities or events that are occurring too often to allow you to have a more positive quality of life. You must also understand that you can choose the kinds of activities and events in which you engage. In fact, you have always chosen (to a large extent) the kinds of events and activities in which you engage. You will see that you are able to choose different events and activities if you want, especially those that will increase your quality of life. At its basis, behavior is directed toward trying to create the most positive set of experiences possible. How well this is accomplished will determine our satisfaction or disappointment with our lives. Simply turning your attention to these experiences will increase your awareness of how to increase the number of positive experiences you can expect. You do **not** need to fill your day with 24 hours of positive experiences to have a high quality of life. You simply have to have more positive experiences per day than you have negative experiences. This may turn out to be only three or four positive experiences per day as long as the negative experiences are fewer and as long as the positive experiences outweigh the negative experiences to you.

In addition to activities as a source of positive (or negative) experiences, there are two other important sources. We have hinted at the first of these two. The first of these is events you attend or are exposed to. Events in our lives can produce positive experiences, such as being taken to a show to see a movie, or they can be negative events, such as being physically abused. The second source of negative or positive experience is yourself - namely, your self-concept as transferred into your "self-talk." Everyone thinks about themselves, thinks about their lives, and thinks about the activities and events they have in their lives. We describe this thinking as "self-talk." Self-talk itself can be negative or positive and it can be rational or irrational. That is, we could say negative things about ourselves, such as "I'm not very attractive," but that could be an irrational thought. In fact, you could be quite attractive, but your irrational negative thinking makes you have a negative experience when you think about yourself. Self-talk is such a strong influence on our quality of life that it is essential to include in this segment. Our self descriptors are a powerful source of subjective experience. We can view ourselves in positive terms such as capable, attractive, intelligent, or resourceful; or we can view ourselves in such negative words as useless, clumsy, dumb, or unattractive. These words serve to produce self-generated experiences of a positive or negative nature. Our self-talk will also cause us to interpret events in our lives either positively or negatively. So, for example, a person with a low opinion of himself or herself will view the world as foreboding and unmanageable, whereas a person with a positive self concept will see the world as an opportunity that is manageable. The end result is that we can produce our own pleasurable, successful, and meaningful experiences mentally. Or we can produce distressing, painful, and isolating experiences mentally. Taken together, these three sources - activities, events, and self talk - determine our experiences. The idea that experience is the final common result of our actions and behavior can also be seen clearly in cases of mental illness. For example, a person with paranoid delusions is behaving consistently in relation to what he or she experiences, not in relation to what is objectively true. The person who is severely depressed also responds to his or her life by describing it as negative and painful. Patients of mine who have been severely depressed responded to events and activities very negatively, whereas "objectively" these activities and events would not be interpreted as negatively by someone who is not depressed or by the same person after their depression was improved. Since their future behavior is directed by what they experience, sometimes it is so painful that people think the only way to feel better is not to feel at all; that is, to consider suicide.

We frequently hear of mass shootings at schools or offices where the shooter kills several people. These shooters are generally operating from their own intense experience of how they view the situation and themselves. Their experience becomes so negative and strong that they take whatever desperate action they think or feel is necessary. So, for example, a shooting in a school recently was done by a freshman student who had built up an intense experience of rage in response to being bullied, and expressing the rage took the form of shooting classmates. It is not that he was bullied that caused the shooting; it was that he became so enraged by the bullying. In other words, his own inner interpretation of what the bullying meant to him and what he needed to do about it was due to his own internal self-talk, which itself was irrational and outwardly directed. When all is said and done, it is the subjective experience of individuals, whether mentally ill or mentally well, that counts the most in determining their behavior and therefore, ultimately, their quality of life.

QUALITY OF LIFE

The role of what we have described as self-talk, or your characteristic way of thinking about important issues in your life, including your view of yourself, your situation, and your future, is important for two additional reasons. First, people are usually unaware of their own thinking habits. Just as a fish doesn't know it's in water because it has never been out of water for a comparison, we often don't recognize our own thinking style because we have not explored other ways of thinking about ourselves, our situation, or our future. We may believe that other people think exactly like we do, or we may believe that what we think is normal given our circumstances. However, our own thinking may set limits on our ability to increase our quality of life because of two important facts. First, our thinking may be irrational in the sense that it is not completely accurate. For example, while we may believe that the future will never get better, this very thought may prevent us from trying because if it can never get better, why try? We must examine our thinking, often with counseling help, to see if we are misconstruing our views. Second, how we think can keep our quality of life lower than it would otherwise be because most of us don't want to venture into situations or activities that are too different from our view of ourselves. Thus a young person who is not an experienced dancer may avoid social situations that could improve his quality of life because he views that there may be dancing involved and he doesn't want to be embarrassed. He is missing the fact that he can always improve his dancing and that there are benefits to him for attending social events, and he is limiting his own range of activities inappropriately.

CHAPTER 12: GETTING STARTED

There are three ways, in general, to increase the number of positive experiences in your life. The first way to increase the number of positive experiences you have is to increase the number of positive activities in which you engage. But remember, positive experiences come in three forms: pleasurable ones, successful ones, and meaningful ones. For example, if you find that when you have volunteered to help others it made you feel good then perhaps you should consider increasing the number of these meaningful activities, not only to help others, but also to enhance your own QOL. Then it is simply a matter of finding out who you most like to help. This could include individual organizations helping children, older adults, animal shelters, etc.

The second way is to increase the variety of the positive activities in which you engage, having sufficient pleasurable, successful, and meaningful experiences rather than being limited to mostly one or two of these kinds. If you focus on only a particular experience and the activities that produce it, you run the risk of becoming one-sided and limiting the available alternatives as you grow older. Successful executives who derive their quality of life from their positions, admiration from others, and material possessions, may feel lost when it comes time to retire. Without a source of other positive experiences to take place of their successful experiences, these people may feel lost when they need to retire instead of having a cartful of meaningful, purposeful, or pleasurable activities in which to engage. There may be little else to maintain a high QOL. Many professionals find themselves in this bind, especially physicians, dentists, and businessmen. When the feelings of success, achievement, and admiration are lost, psychological and physical problems often abound. It is well-known that when one's sources of connection and support disappear, life expectancy is greatly diminished.

The third way is to allow yourself to recognize and acknowledge all aspects of the positive experience (its feeling component, its cognitive component, its behavioral component, and its physiological component) that occur when you are involved in various activities, events, or self-talk. In other words, extract as much positiveness as you can from each activity or event. Squeeze as much juice from the orange as you can. However, this extraction process requires you to slow down a little in order to fully capture the experience. One cannot go through life at a fast pace and expect to experience all the positiveness that life can bring. You should allow yourself time to fully experience what you are involved in. How does it feel? What do you think as you are involved in it? How does your body react when you are involved in these things? What is your behavior like? If we use the compass of examining these four areas, we will find out what activities and events really lead us to have positive responses and which ones don't. When you find the positive ones, either that you select or that just come your way, you extract as much positivity as you can. To illustrate this point with a "messy" example, imagine you are going out to dinner for barbeque at a new restaurant you heard about. You could just go and eat the meal and maybe savor the sauces a little bit without extracting as much positive experience as is available to you there. On the other hand, you could learn a little bit more about the restaurant, how long it's been in business, who the owners are, etc.; you could lather up the ribs with more sauce and really dig into them and savor the taste and the texture in your mouth; you could notice the fullness or the satisfaction you get from eating; and you could express to your dinner partner what you like most about the dinner. This way, you are extracting more elements of the positive experience than simply sitting down to have a meal and leaving afterwards. I hope this gives you a sense of what I mean.

Pleasurable, Successful, and Meaningful Event Schedules

People sometimes need assistance to identify pleasurable, successful, or meaningful activities in which they might engage. You may think of it as strange that you can't identify such activities, but reassure yourself that most people cannot. Again, these activities are important only as far as they promote positive experiences in you that in turn lead to higher quality of life. We have provided examples of these various activities in the appendix. These schedules are to be used as tools for suggestion of different kinds of activities. Hopefully, they will stimulate you to think of others as well. Appendices C, D, and E list various activities that fall into these categories as judged by a group of raters. However, you might judge some of these activities to fall under a different category (e.g. you might judge being at the beach more meaningful than pleasurable, and that is perfectly alright).

Remember that pleasurable activities also include the following: joy, excitement, fun, novelty, happiness, gratification, delight, etc. Successful activities refer to those bringing a sense of achievement, accomplishment, recognition, or satisfaction. Meaningful activities include those providing a sense of purpose, importance, fulfillment, spirituality, belonging, etc. Please use these schedules to help you, but not limit you to, activities that will lead to the kinds of experiences that underlie a positive QOL. These three schedules can be used in comparison to the Positive and Negative Experiences Inventories that you took earlier. If you did not have an abundance of positive experiences compared to negative ones when you filled out the inventories, then these three additional schedules should be especially beneficial for you. They are not designed to tell you how to reduce negative experiences. That will come later. These are designed to help you increase your positive experiences.

What Would It Take?

Here we will focus on another general technique that can be helpful to you in using a self-guided method. In this technique, you will be asked to direct your own program of self-improvement. This will not interfere with the techniques described above and below, but will blend in with them. We have previously stated that you need to increase the positive and/or decrease the negative experiences. Here you get a chance to identify and work on some of those positive or negative experiences. You are probably the best person to identify what it would take to improve your QOL. For now, answer the following questions:

Whatever level of QOL you currently have, what would it take to move you one step higher? For example, if you are currently at QOL "0" or neutral, what would it take to move you one unit higher? What you identify here is very important. You should give it considerable thought. It may be one of the positive experiences that you wish to increase, or it may be one of the negative experiences you wish to decrease.

What are the appropriate resources to help you accomplish this change in QOL? If what you want happens to be the reduction of a negative experience, we will cover that in a subsequent chapter. If, on the other hand, what you mentioned is to increase something positive, then it matters what kinds of positive experiences you are lacking.

If you are lacking enough pleasurable experiences and cannot think of anything you might think enjoyable, you can turn to Appendix C. This appendix contains a pleasurable event schedule. This schedule contains many activities that are potentially pleasurable and enjoyable for you. Look them over and see if there are items and activities that interest you and are feasible for you to do. Don't wait until you feel better to try them; start trying some right away. If you lack sufficient successful experiences and feel that you are not achieving enough, it is likely that you either don't have a goal in mind (short term or long term) or that you lack a plan or motivation to accomplish it.

Appendix F describes a goal attainment procedure that will help you attain what you state would improve your QOL. If you have no goals, please see the instructions under your level of QOL. In order to help you help yourself and move a little closer to your desired QOL, we have included a Goal Attainment Schedule (GAS) for your use. The GAS is designed to help you achieve that goal. Once achieved, you can do it again and again to further increase your QOL. Your QOL will increase because whatever you have stated above will translate into more positive and fewer negative experiences once it is achieved. So, if you identified that it was a job you desired, the job is good in itself because it supplies an income and benefits. However, it also increases the positive experiences of having a meaningful role, a sense of success, interactions with other people, and provides some control over your future.

This section has focused on the general idea of ways to improve and increase your overall positive experiences in life, which will then increase your QOL. It has not focused on what to do about negative experiences. As an overall strategy, we would like to increase positive experiences while decreasing negative experiences. Techniques for reducing negative experiences will be explained in a later chapter.

Personality Characteristics and QOL

Another general step towards improving your QOL is to help you use your personality characteristics to improve your QOL or to determine if you have personality characteristics that are standing in your way for improving your QOL. By personality we mean long standing traits or characteristics that describe you. These are not unchangeable characteristics but represent a few that you should know about in regards to your own quality of life. Hundreds of personality traits, characteristics, and factors have been described over the last hundred years in the psychological and psychiatric literature. We are going to focus on very few of them, however. In fact, we are going to focus on only five. These five have a direct bearing on your ability to change your QOL. These five have the interesting acronym of "**BOOMS**". We hope this acronym makes it easier for you to remember these traits. Perhaps you can think of them as booming out loud to you as important characteristics you should try to maintain or change. **B** stands for how strongly you **believe** you have control over your life, yourself, and the future. This means you believe you can change your circumstances and that you also have some control over yourself and the future. **O** stands for your **optimism** in life. Optimism refers to your characteristic view of whether things are likely to turn out good or not. The second **O** refers to **openness** to experience. Openness to experience means how many parts of the experience "molecules" you allow yourself to have, and whether you are open to new activities and events in your life. **M** stands for **motivation**. Motivation means your willingness to try even in the face of difficulty and hardship. **S** stands for **seeking** advice. Do you actively seek and use advice from experts to improve your situation, or, instead, do you wait for things to get better or try to do everything by yourself?

Below, in Figure 12.1, you will find a diagram containing these five personality traits. For each trait, you are asked to rate yourself (be honest) on a scale ranging from "like me" to "not like me". The mid-point is neither like you, nor not like you. There are also gradations that you can see on the diagram. These include "somewhat like me" and "mostly like me". For each trait, circle the answer as it applies to you. Now, choose someone you are especially close to, such as your spouse or partner, and have them rate you. If you two disagree, please discuss the reasons and make a final choice on the scale. Take the personality profile before reading further.

Figure 12.1

BOOMS Personality Profile

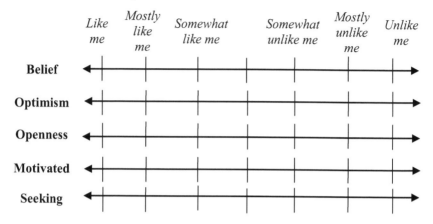

We are now going to discuss the importance of each of these traits in relation to attaining and maintaining a high QOL. We will take each of the traits in order. Look at your diagram and connect each of the circled items. Now, which items, if any, are to the right of the mid-line? How many are far to the right of the mid-line (that is, "mostly unlike me" or "unlike me")? Any items that are on the right hand side could be problematic for you in terms of being barriers that you impose on yourself that prevent you from attaining as high QOL as possible. These traits may not allow you to have as high a QOL as you might have, if they are on the right hand side. On the other hand, if your scores are on the left hand side of the mid-line, these personality traits can serve as a real asset for you in promoting your QOL. All of the personality traits are modifiable.

Now look at how your friend or partner rated you. Discuss any differences between you two, and decide on the final point. These traits, because they are learned, can also be unlearned. It will take a change in your everyday experiences and effort on your part to look at things differently.

Belief: Believing you can control or influence your life is very important. There are three main beliefs that are important. First is the belief that you have some control over your current situation. Your current situation is, to some extent, a product of choices you have made in the past and choices you are currently making. Where you are in life is not predetermined nor is it the result of random acts. One way to improve your life is to make different decisions and different choices about your activities, the events you attend, or your self-talk than ones you have made in the past. There is virtually nothing that cannot be improved. But you need to believe that you have at least some control over these things. To a large extent, you must view yourself as a cause of your life. For example, losing your temper with others is a choice and it may impair your QOL as others retreat from you physically and emotionally. However, losing your temper is a choice and you can choose to do something different. You could take more time to consider the facts and you could think about what you are trying to accomplish by losing your temper, or you could think about the impact on your larger relationship with the other person and decide losing your temper is not the right thing to do. As another example, you can choose to do different things on the weekends, instead of the same old things. Let yourself branch out and do something that you normally wouldn't do and break loose from old habits.

Beliefs also extend to what you think about the future. If you believe you have little control, then you also have little hope that the future will be better than at present. However, the future can be shaped in a variety of ways from this point forward if you believe that you have a lot of control over that process. Research shows that people have about 50% control over major outcomes in their life, such as the job they eventually get, who they eventually marry, where they eventually live, and how much education they eventually obtain. However, people are generally capable of having between 60% to 70% control over what they **experience** in life regardless of their circumstances.

Finally, beliefs extend to yourself and your view of yourself, which we said we call self-concept. Your self-concept is a set of beliefs. Those beliefs may be true, partially true, or false. Only self-awareness and feedback from others can answer this question. The words you use to describe yourself express to others your self-concept. Your self-concept sets limits on what you are willing to try or not try. If you view yourself in negative terms, such as stupid, inept, socially undesirable, or timid, you will live within the boundaries of these self descriptions. You will consider any instances of normal interactions that seem to reflect on this as confirming your viewpoint. This is totally irrational! Views of yourself are choices and beliefs that you have. A belief is not a fact. It is an assumption or a hypothesis or a guess about the way things are, but it is not a fact. These irrational beliefs will lead to a lower QOL because one of two things will probably happen. One possibility is that a negative view of yourself will limit your activities and exposure to new events to where very few are available to you. The other possibility is that you will engage in normal activities but interpret your experiences as negative rather than positive. For example, if you go to a party, you might come away worrying whether you made mistakes at the party rather than focusing on the good times you had. Negative beliefs about yourself will shape the kind of experience that you derive from the activity. Since about ninety percent of people have pretty much a normal personality with a combination of strengths and weaknesses, instead of focusing on your weaknesses, choose to focus on your strengths and develop those more. And unless you have a glaring personality disorder, other people will more or less ignore your weaknesses because they fall within a normal range.

Consequently, people who believe they have little control over themselves or their situations are likely to turn around and blame their negative experiences on others and on their situations. They may try to change others in the mistaken belief that it will reduce their own negative experiences. However, in this book, you are solely focusing on yourself and what you can do to reduce your negative experiences. If you blame your foul mood on how your spouse acts, you will not only be wrong (because no one can make you feel something) but you will also create more negative interactions for yourself.

Optimism: The second element on the personality profile reflects optimism, which is also something like a belief, but it's also like an attitude. An attitude is a core belief that cuts across multiple situations. In this case, optimism means that the person has a basic core belief that, with effort, events will turn out well. A person who is not optimistic is said to be pessimistic. Their underlying attitude is that, regardless of what they try or the effort they put out, events will not turn out well. For example, if you indicated that being optimistic is not like you, that could present a problem to improving your QOL. Being pessimistic is usually inappropriate and is usually based upon faulty beliefs and limited facts. There is nearly always something that can be done to improve a situation, even if it is just reconstructing the way you look at the situation. Even if you are told you have a terminal illness, you have control over how you will deal with it. That is what we mean by the idea that you always have something you can do to improve the situation. A pessimistic attitude will almost guarantee that you have low QOL because 1) you will not be able to fully appreciate positive experiences, 2) you will be looking for the next negative experiences to confirm your negative view point, and 3) people around you will get tired of you and withdraw their support.

Openness: Openness to experience means both allowing yourself to experience life more fully and your willingness to experience new things, including those slightly beyond your "comfort zone." As you may recall, experiencing life fully means that you have, and recognize, physical, emotional, cognitive, and behavioral reactions to significant activities and events. This morning, I was enjoying a nice breakfast with eggs and toast. I could have just hurried through it to get on to my next activity for the day, but I always allow myself an extra ten minutes for breakfast in order to thoroughly enjoy it. With each bite I enjoy the flavors and the texture of what I'm eating. I also recall the many times in the past I had breakfast like this and with whom I was dining. Having breakfast like this makes me feel good and it prepares me for the next activities of the day. This way, I have already gotten myself a good amount of positive experience, and as I go through the day, I will be looking for a variety of additional positive experiences. Infants and young children are strongly driven to explore and are open to new experiences as long as they are not frightened or hurt by them (i.e. as long as it's within or close to their comfort zone). Adults should strive to be like most children when it comes to openness to experience. They should try to recognize as many of the four elements of experience as they can from every event and activity. They should also be willing to open themselves up to new events and activities that are not too far outside their comfort zone in order to increase the number and variety of experiences they receive.

Motivation: In the context of QOL, the term motivation is used primarily to describe your willingness to try and to persevere. These are two separate elements. The first refers to motivation to begin something, like an exercise program. The second refers to your ability to persist in it and keep going even when faced with setbacks or slow progress. Highly motivated people not only decide to start a new activity or new direction in life, but they do not allow barriers to stand in their way. They are persistent. They find a way to overcome barriers or get around barriers in order to achieve their goal. People with low motivation tend to start the same number of activities but give up when the going gets tough. You can see this behavior in what is called "the New Year resolution phenomenon." Many people make New Year resolutions to start doing something or stop doing something else, such as an exercise program or to stop smoking. And they do either with great conviction. However, around March or April, most people are not following their New Year resolutions because of the difficulties, demands, or changes that are required in order to keep a resolution in other parts of their lives. If you are motivated to improve something about yourself, you must be willing to deal with the costs of what it would take, not only to start a program, but to maintain it months later. Being willing to start a program, versus maintaining a program, are two different things. Improving your QOL is going to require you to do both elements. If you are going to improve your QOL, you are going to need to change some of your current activities.

This may not be easy, because your current activities are over-learned. As such, even though they don't help you, you are comfortable with them. Because there are only so many hours in a day, you will have to stop doing some of those things in order to start doing some new things. You need to keep doing these newer things in order to improve your QOL.

Seeking: A wise person uses experts as consultants to gather advice and recommendations on how to improve something, whether it is a golf swing or how to cure a medical problem. When you use experts' advice and consultations, it doesn't mean you are putting others in charge of yourself. Instead, you, as the chief executive officer of Y.O.U., Inc., are assembling a team of experts to assist you, while you take control and maintain the right of a final decision. If you instead try to solve distressing problems or to develop new positive experiences by yourself, you are limited by your own knowledge, experience, and perspective. If you passively wait for things to get better, the most likely scenario is that nothing will change. As a team leader, think about what kinds of experts whose advice you need. Who will help you to improve your QOL? Do you need, for example, a close friend who can serve as confidant to allow you to express your feelings and thoughts about subjects and to receive feedback? Do you need a physician to help you with a medical problem? Do you need a trainer to help you with an exercise program? Do you need a social worker to help you through the bureaucratic maze? Do you need a librarian to direct you to the source of information? Whatever members you need on your team, start to put them together and add what is missing. If you are trying to solve a major problem in your life, you may need professional help from different disciplines. These experts are often available free of charge if you have low income, are available under insurance coverage, or are available for reasonable fees if paid privately. If you are trying to resolve a relatively minor problem, then there are probably people around you who can give you advice and feedback about what you are trying to do. It is always good to get at least one other person's perspective on what it is you are trying to accomplish because we invariably omit one or two important ingredients if left to our own limited thinking. People who improve their quality of life the most are those who seek and use resources and advice from others. People who either do not, or refuse to, seek and use advice will find advancement to go much slower.

Obviously, these five personality traits interact with each other. They can interact in a positive way or in a negative way. Let's take an example of how they might interact negatively. Suppose you score low on both **B**elief and **M**otivation. Let's say further that your belief about yourself is that you have never been good at sports, having found them too strenuous for you. Let's also say, though, that you want to start an exercise program to lose a little weight, firm up your body, and have a healthier life style. You start an exercise program and you were doing well at the beginning. However, after three months you don't see a lot of improvement, frequent exercise makes your muscles sore, and no one is telling you how great you look. You are beginning to think, "this is difficult" and "I've never been good at sports." The chances you persevere and continue with your exercise program are now very slight. No external rewards are coming forth, and difficulties imposed by the exercise just support your self- view that you are not an athlete. Your beliefs are undermining your motivation. If you could change your belief about yourself to one that says "I'm pretty normal and this is what most people go through," you will be more likely to keep going. Also if you thought about it at the beginning, just three months is not long enough to make a difference. You need to have a regular exercise program for at least 6 to 9 months to get the kinds of changes you are looking for.

So you can see how your beliefs about yourself and your situations of exercising interact with each other. The same can be said of other personality traits and how they interact. If you are not very optimistic, why would you believe you have control over your future? On the other hand, if you are optimistic, you probably will persevere longer at a task because you believe that will eventually lead to a good outcome. One of the main messages to be taken away from this section is that these personality traits are important but they are modifiable. It may take help from somebody else to point out your own fallacies and irrationalities, but these traits can all be made more adaptable.

Take another look at your personality profile now. Pay attention to scores that are only on the right hand side of the mid-line. I am going to give you a rule that you should take seriously in examining your score. If any score on the right hand side is under the heading "unlike me" **or** if any 2 scores on the right hand side are under the column "mostly unlike me" **or** if any 3 scores on the right hand side are under the heading "somewhat unlike me", there is a problem. The problem is that a major source of your low QOL is the negative experiences you create for yourself. These scores mean that you cannot have many high scores on the left hand side of the mid-line. Instead, you are somewhat or even largely possessing traits that are undermining your own efforts at improvement. For example, if you scored "mostly unlike me" on the trait of Seeking assistance, that means you actually resist advice and assistance when it is in your best interest to get it. What is lying behind your recalcitrant attitude regarding advice from others? Do you think they can take control of you? Do you not trust them? Do you think you are the sharpest knife in a drawer? Whatever the cause, it's probably not helping you. Similarly, if you scored "unlike me" on the trait of Optimism, then you are truly pessimistic. Therefore, you will lack motivation to initiate new actions, will make despairing remarks to people who try to help you, and not trust the result if something turns out well. Again, this is a learned trait and needs to be unlearned as quickly as possible, so you will stop damaging yourself. I suggest you follow up by reading one of the resources suggested for this chapter as listed in the last chapter of the book.

On the other hand, if all of your scores were to the left of the mid-line or if only one score is in the "somewhat not like me" category, you have many positive traits that are probably already adding to your quality of life. However, if we can rule out that your personal traits are not interfering with your quality of life, some of the other recommendations and suggestions in this book will probably still be of value to you.

Summary of General Principle

In summary, this chapter has dealt with general principles concerning improving your QOL. It has emphasized the importance of increasing the frequency of positive experiences in your life while diminishing the number of negative experiences. Because most experiences are derived through our activities and exposure to certain events, we also proposed that you examine the kinds of activities in which you engage. Activities have been divided into three kinds: those that are likely to provide a sense of pleasure, fun, or enjoyment; those that are likely to provide a sense of achievement, accomplishment, or success; and those that are likely to provide a sense of meaning, purpose, or belonging. People who have a high QOL usually have a combination of all three kinds of experiences, and they therefore engage in activities and events that sustain all those types of experiences. People with a low QOL either have a very low number of these positive experiences or their positive experiences are limited to just one or two categories (such as just focused on pleasure or success). Having enough positive experiences is also dependent upon **allowing** yourself to have these experiences. We described five personality traits that could stand in the way of achieving a higher QOL, because they act as restrainers on your experiences. We also described another procedure to help you increase your own QOL by asking yourself what it would take to move one unit higher on the QOL scale. This will either involve reducing some negative experiences or increasing some positive experiences. Here, the goal attainment schedule can be helpful in formulating your own plan for how to improve your QOL.

SPECIFIC STEPS FOR INCREASING QOL

CHAPTER 13: STEP BY STEP BY STEP

In the previous chapter, we described several general principles involved in improving your QOL. These principles included focusing on experiences, increasing positive experiences, decreasing negative experiences, developing a plan to improve your QOL by one unit or half a unit, and examining some personality traits that may stand in your way of improving your QOL. In the current chapter, we will focus on specific steps you can take to improve your QOL that depend upon your current level. The steps and principles recommended for one level of QOL will not be the same as those recommended for a different level of QOL. We will begin with lower QOL scores and move toward higher QOL scores. We will be using your converted QOL score, which, as you will recall, can range from -3 through 0 to +3. By the end of 6 months, we expect your QOL score to be one unit higher. At the end of 9 months, we expect it to be 2 units higher. You can continue after that to further improve your own QOL.

A score of -3

As you will recall from Chapter 6, a score of -3 means that you are experiencing great distress. This distress can manifest itself physically, psychologically, or interpersonally. Despite how badly you feel, if you follow the recommended steps below you can expect to feel significantly better in approximately 1 month. You can only gain from this point and you can expect to gain significantly over this month and beyond. You may need to dig deep down and search for the last bit of motivation to help yourself, but it will be worth it. If you don't do anything you could stay where you are for a very long time. In a sense, I am surprised that you are even reading this book because of how badly you feel.

At this time we must divide your program of improvement into two parts. The first part has to do with getting treatment, or better treatment, for the underlying problems that are causing your distress. Once that is accomplished and your QOL score moves up to approximately -1, we can concentrate on improving your QOL further until it becomes actually positive. However, for now we need to concentrate on the most fundamental problems. Here are the recommended steps:

1) Review your scores on the Positive Experiences Inventory and Negative Experiences Inventory. Ideally, there should be at least two to three times more positive experiences than negative experiences. You will notice that you have the reverse. You probably have approximately three times as many negative experiences as you have positive experiences. This is a sure-fire recipe for severe distress and physical problems.

2) Research shows that you have a 90% chance of having a depressive disorder. Even if you have a physical illness or disability, the depression is making it much worse. Turn to Appendix G of this book and look for the questionnaire labeled Kemp Depression Assessment Questionnaire. Read the instructions, answer the

questions, and then add up your score. You can also interpret your score by the guideline provided. It is absolutely imperative that you seek assistance if you obtained a score indicating that you have moderate to major depression.

3) Make an appointment with your primary care doctor to discuss how you are feeling both emotionally and physically. Take the result of the Depression Assessment Questionnaire with you to the doctor so the two of you can discuss the result. If depression is not the major contributor to your distress, your doctor can look for physical causes for your distress. If depression is a principle cause of your distress, most physicians are comfortable starting you on an appropriate medication. He or she may want to refer you to a psychiatrist but don't be alarmed. Psychiatrists today are experts on which medicine to give to an individual who is stressed and worn out. If you are a candidate for medication, it usually takes 4 to 8 weeks for the medicine to begin to help. At the end of 8 weeks, if you are taking the proper medication, you will already begin to feel better.

4) In all probability, you need both medication and counseling to help you feel better. The stress in your life has become so great that it has affected you physically, all the way down to how certain nerves in your body work. Medicines help to restore the normal balance to these nerves. However, medicine alone cannot teach you different coping techniques, nor provide the support you need right now. Therefore, you also need a personal counselor, whether it is a social worker, psychologist, clergy, or other licensed professionals. A close friend, in this case, is not sufficient as a counselor. You may need as few as 4 sessions with a counselor or as many as 12 to see an improvement.

5) Follow the advice of your primary care provider, psychiatrist, and personal counselor, and do not give up hope. In approximately 2 months you will move from QOL of -3 to QOL of -2, which will be a big improvement.

6) Each day, try to do two or three things you find enjoyable, and two or three things that you can accomplish successfully, even if each is a small task. If you have difficulty identifying pleasurable activities or activities that give you a sense of accomplishment, turn to the Appendix C (Pleasurable Event Schedule) and Appendix D (Successful Event Schedule). It will give you many suggestions regarding activities you might consider. Keep track of how you feel after you have done something enjoyable or successful. Gradually increase the number of times each week that you do these things or other things like them.

7) Your doctor, your counselor and you will probably focus on negative experiences in your life. After about one month you will notice that you are now gradually decreasing negative experiences of life and increasing positive experiences. That is exactly what you need.

8) Also examine Appendix E (Meaningful Event Schedule). Most people under severe stress find little meaning or purpose in their lives. However, these are very important experiences to have and to hold dear. See if any of the activities listed in Appendix E appeal to you to help you feel the spiritual or otherwise meaningful desire that most of us have. If you can find meaning or anything positive about the distressing times you are going through, that itself can help you deal with the distress.

9) During these difficult times, confide in a close friend. Pick

someone who will not judge you or find fault with you as you go through these difficult days. Find someone who is supportive and well-adjusted. Research shows that the presence of at least one "confidant" during the time of stress is of a great value.

10) Read Chapter 17 on managing stress and reducing negative experiences. It is a synopsis of what we currently know about managing stress of any kind.

11) Avoid stressful or negative events as much as you can for the next couple of months. This includes avoiding people you find annoying, avoiding movies that are violent or disturbing, and avoiding other things you find unpleasant or potentially disturbing.

12) As you move up the QOL scale, follow the recommendation corresponding to that level in order to keep your progress going forward. That is, when you retake the QOL scale, when you get to a -2 score, follow the direction listed below for the -2 score.

A score of -2

If you scored -2 on the converted scale, there is a 50% chance that you have some form of a depressive disorder or medical disorder causing you undue distress. If you have a depressive disorder, it may or may not require medication but it certainly requires some counseling to assist you. The steps listed below are designed to help you improve your QOL from the current level to a +1 over the next 10 months. By carefully following the steps, you can reasonably expect to be feeling and functioning much better fairly soon.

1) Please follow the first 6 recommended steps under a score of -3 (see previous section).

2) You will notice that, at the present time, you have more negative experiences than positive experiences. This pattern needs to be reversed. After pleasurable activities, activities that provide you a sense of accomplishment, control, and success are the next most important in which to engage. You probably feel that you are not making much progress in life. Therefore, you lack the positive experiences that go with being successful. Start with even the simplest of tasks that you have been putting off (such as cleaning up a room). Focus on getting that done without being distracted by other projects. You will be surprised by how good you feel.

3) Continue with your counseling. It is likely you will only need 6 to 8 sessions.

4) As you continue to make improvements on the number of positive experiences in life and decrease the number of negative experiences, you can consider adding some meaningful activities to your life. If you have difficulty coming up with these activities, you can find a short list of them in Appendix E.

5) As you move up the QOL scale, read the recommended steps that correspond to that level.

6) Your desire to increase your quality of life is admirable, but at times it will be difficult. There may be some setbacks along the way, but try not to get too discouraged. You can keep these setbacks to a short period and you **will** gradually improve your quality of life.

A score of -1

If you scored at this level, you still have slightly more negative experiences in your life overall than positive experiences.

The chances that you have a true depressive disorder are low; probably only a 10% chance. However, at the same time, you are probably struggling with one or two major issues in your life (such as your health or marriage) and you feel (or fear) you are not winning the struggle yet. This means you still have many unresolved issues and feelings that are getting in the way of having a more positive life. It is possible to lead a much more satisfactory life and experience a higher QOL by following the suggestions below. You should be able to change your score from a -1 to +1 in the next 4 to 8 months by following these recommended steps.

1) You could strongly benefit from a counselor, whether a licensed professional, a member of clergy, or your personal physician. You probably only need 6 to 8 sessions of counseling to learn a better way of coping with the things that are causing you distress now. Your counselor needs to be a professional and not someone who is a friend of yours.

2) You can take the Depression Assessment Questionnaire in Appendix G if you like, but it is doubtful that you will score really high right now. What might be more illuminating is to take the Life Satisfaction Questionnaire that you will find in Appendix H. This scale is helpful in targeting areas of life that are presenting difficulties. Try to focus on what kinds of negative experiences are being generated in areas you rate low for satisfaction. The next chapter will help you to formulate plans for dealing with these negative experiences. These areas of dissatisfaction are also ones you should discuss with your professional counselor.

3) Review your scores on the BOOMS questionnaire and see if any of those traits are potential barriers to improving your QOL.

4) Now you have several useful pieces of information that particularly address reasons for your negative experiences. These include your doctor's opinion of any underlying medical issues, the Positive and Negative Experiences Inventories, the Life Satisfaction Questionnaire, and your BOOMS profile. This is ample information for you and your counselor to go over to identify the causes of your negative experiences. You can also look at the section on Managing Negative Experiences.

5) You and your counselor can focus on reasons for, and improvements in, your negative experiences. You can simultaneously start to increase your positive experiences. You don't need to wait until your negative experiences are well diminished to start adding more positive experiences to your life. If you need further assistance to increase your positive experiences, look at Appendices C, D, and E. These appendices contain suggestions of various activities you might consider for increasing (or trying to increase) the total number of positive experiences in your life.

6) As you progress to higher levels of QOL, read recommendations that go with each of these levels.

7) Retake the QOL scale, the Positive Experiences Inventory and the Negative Experiences Inventory every 6 weeks and monitor your progress. Improvements on the QOL scale of .5 or better are significant improvements. So you might find yourself going from -1 to -.5 and then on to neutral or 0.

A score of 0

You have a unique problem. You are neither happy nor

unhappy; neither satisfied nor dissatisfied. You seem to be just existing. Perhaps you feel a little lost or you don't know what direction to take. Maybe you are waiting for something or someone to come along and lead you or direct you rather than directing and leading yourself. You probably did not endorse many personality traits indicating that they are like you. You may also feel yourself being pulled in too many different directions. In an odd kind of way, your score indicates that you may have the most difficulty increasing your QOL. Although your score is in the middle of the QOL scale, you actually are below average compared to others because you have more negative than positive experiences. Nevertheless, you can increase your QOL. You can probably go from your current score to +2 within 6 to 10 months. Here are some recommended steps.

1) Examine the scores on the Positive and Negative Experiences Inventories. Now look at the Positive Experiences Inventory only. What proportion of your answers are in each of the three categories? You probably have a low number in each category (less than 15 total and 3 or less in the meaningful category). These scores indicate you need commitment and direction in your life. Other people probably find you indecisive or low on motivation.

2) You seem to be handling distress in your life fairly well. Distress is not overwhelming for you, and you manage to cope well most of the time.

3) Now examine your Negative Experiences Inventory. You probably have more negative experiences than positive experiences. It's difficult to say for sure, but your negative experiences are most likely interpersonal and psychological. If so, your psychological issues are spilling over to affect you interpersonally.

4) Your strategy needs to include reducing the number of negative experiences in your life while increasing the positive experiences in your life.

5) Go back to the section that describes the difference between experience and activity (Ch. 11). Practice letting yourself experience things in all four of the ways described there.

6) Gradually work on increasing the number of positive experiences each week. Especially focus on social activities which are the area where you are probably below the norm in terms of how much you interact with others.

7) Reexamine your scores on the personality profile. Be careful to notice any scores that are to the right of the center line. These traits may underlie the reason that you don't have a higher QOL right now. Do not minimize the importance of these traits. If you believe that any of them are causing you difficulties, discuss it with your counselor to understand them better and to hopefully change them.

8) A key positive experience for you will be finding something that you find meaningful, of great value, or something you can build a passion about. This will help set a lot of other things in line for you.

9) Retake the QOL scale, the Positive Experiences Inventory and the Negative Experiences Inventory every six weeks and monitor your progress. Improvements on the QOL scale of .5 or better are significant improvements. As you get to the next level higher, follow the directions for that level. Please remember to note the date.

CHAPTER 14: STEP BY STEP CONTINUED

This chapter is devoted primarily to scores of +1, +2 and +3. The common denominator across these scores is that all of them have more positive experiences than negative experiences on a consistent basis. The recommended steps in this chapter will focus both on further reducing negative experiences and suggestions for increasing positive experiences. The ultimate goal is not just to have a positive ratio of these kinds of experiences, but to begin to show that people ultimately have control over their experiences. Therefore they have the ability to create experiences in the way they would like to have them. Methods for doing so are included in the chapter on general steps, in this chapter, and hidden among the parts of various other chapters.

A score of +1

You are doing well in terms of QOL. You score about average compared to everyone else. Your quality of life is slightly positive. You have more positive experiences than negative experiences, and other people probably see you as successful and happy. Scores of +1 are often found among people who are very busy and concentrating on making progress in their lives. For example, this score is common among medical students and graduate students. There is still room for improvement however. And you should be able to increase your QOL up to a +2 or maybe even a +3 within the next 6 to 10 months by following these recommended steps.

1) Examine your scores on the inventories for positive and negative experiences and note the total scores as well as the scores for each category. While you have more positive than negative experiences, there is still not a big enough difference between these two scores to give you a higher QOL. In order to achieve a QOL of +2, you need to have approximately one and a half as many positive experiences as you have negative experiences. For example, if you have 10 negative experiences per week, you need 15 or more positive experiences per week on a consistent basis to begin to reach a +2 QOL.

2) Don't forget that these are experiences, not activities or events. If you need to, review the part of this book that describes the difference (Ch. 11).

3) Of the three kinds of positive experiences - pleasurable, successful, and meaningful - which is the most important to you? Is it getting as much time from you as its importance would indicate?

4) Imagine how you can increase the frequency of the category that is most important to you.

5) Now turn that imagined increase into reality by actually doing it. Find time to set aside for engaging in the activities that increase the frequency of the experiences you desire.

6) At the same time, do not decrease the other two kinds of experiences. Instead, maintain the current level or increase them by one or two per week.

7) If you're having difficulty with some negative experiences, there's a section devoted to that topic in this book (Coping With

Negative Experiences).

8) Live your life as though everything is directed toward creating positive experiences for yourself and diminishing negative experiences. That is, begin with the experiences you want to increase or decrease and then think about what activities, events or interactions will help you have those experiences.

9) Monitor your QOL score, Positive Experiences Inventory, and Negative Experiences Inventory by retaking them every six weeks while you rearrange these activities in your life to match up with your desires and values. Remember to note the date on all forms.

A score of +2

If you scored in this category, you are among the top 30% of people in terms of your QOL. You definitely create and have many more positive experiences for yourself than negative experiences. Other people probably see you as successful, efficient, reasonably happy, and well-adjusted. You cope with distress effectively and don't let problems turn into long term sources of distress. There are only a few recommendations that can be made to improve your QOL. You might consider some of the following ideas.

1) Moving from a QOL of +2 to a QOL of +3 is actually a big leap. I suggest you try moving from a QOL of +2 to a QOL of +2.5 first. You will notice that magnitude of difference. Then try going from +2.5 to +3.

2) At this level of QOL, you are beginning to move from improving your QOL by simply having more positive experiences toward extracting more positive experiences from the activities in

which you choose to engage. That is, there will be more of a balance between these two methods of gaining positive experiences.

3) Look at your Positive Experiences Inventory and your Negative Experiences Inventory. People with a QOL of +2 generally have twice as many positive experiences as negative experiences. People with a QOL of +3 generally have three times as many positive experiences as they have negative experiences. But let's face it, there are only so many hours in a day. That's the reason for the advice given above under number 2. If there are only so many activities in which a person can engage to create a positive QOL, then you want to minimize the negative ones and extract as much as possible from the positive ones.

4) Examine the relative balance of pleasurable, successful, and meaningful activities you have during the average week. Are these frequencies the way you would like to have them? Or do you wish that you had more of one kind than you currently have?

5) Typically, people who have scored at your level have an abundance of positive experiences related to pleasure and accomplishment but fewer related to meaning and purpose in their lives. Are you doing as many meaningful activities as you desire or as many meaningful activities as you have time for? The answer to this depends partly on your age. If you are in your 20's or 30's, two to three meaningful activities per week is quite common. As one grows older though, the number of meaningful, purposeful, and value-focused experiences tends to increase by about one per week each decade. Thus, the average 70-year-old who scores a QOL of +2 has a minimum of six meaningful activities/experiences per week, and these may constitute half of the total number of positive experiences they

have that week. In addition, activities they simply enjoyed for the pleasure value in them previously are now seen to also carry a great deal of meaning to them. For example, going out to dinner with friends was perhaps enjoyed because of the good surroundings and the quality of the food. Now, years later, the meaning of the relationship with these other people becomes more important, and spending time with them is valued even if the surroundings are not as fancy as in previous years.

6) If you need suggestions on activities that might increase the amount of meaningful experiences in your life, look at Appendix E and look through the lists of suggested readings and resources.

7) Additionally, take the Social Interaction Inventory (SII) listed in Appendix I. This inventory asks you to indicate how many times in the last week you engaged in certain social, community, or personal activities. Higher scores on the SII are associated with higher scores on QOL. If you score much below the average, consider increasing your social participation. Such participation is associated with pleasure, a sense of accomplishment and success, and meaning according to our research.

8) Examine your Negative Experiences Inventory. Is there one category of negative experiences that stands out the most for you? It could be physical, psychological, or interpersonal. Read the chapter about negative experiences and also seek any additional assistance you need to reduce those negative experiences.

9) Monitor your own level of QOL, Positive Experiences Inventory, and Negative Experiences Inventory every six to eight weeks. As you do, take note of small changes in your QOL. A change of half a unit is very significant when you consider the high level you

are starting from. Please date all forms.

A score of +3

What can I say? You are living a life you find outstanding. Only about 10% of people report their QOL to be this high. Interestingly, high scores like this are found across a wide segment of the population. They include people with major health problems, low as well as high incomes, people with low levels of education as well as high levels of education, people of all ages, and people of all racial/ethnic backgrounds. One of the distinguishing characteristics of people who score a +3 is that they have strong philosophical, spiritual, or meaningful views of themselves, others, and the universe. Most things, if not everything, can be viewed within this context. Because their view point is so broad and spiritualistic, daily problems and stressors do not take on much significance and most of their experiences fit within their very positive views of life, nature, and the universe. A second characteristic of these people is that they grasp the importance of the experiential viewpoint. Regardless of what is going on around them, they focus on drawing as much positive experience from life as possible. Most people in this category of QOL also report that they **create** many of their own experiences. That is, they choose and arrange the activities and events in their lives that will best promote the positive experiences they seek. In addition, many of these people have strong creative trends that are expressed through meditation, music, writing, or the arts. People who score at this level also believe that they have a great deal of control over what happens to them, as well as believing that their reactions to events in life are under their control. However, there are a couple of caveats.

1) You are not off the hook! You now owe it to others to try to tell the story of how you achieved a high QOL using whatever medium you want. For example, you could write an article, write a book, create a painting, create a sculpture, make a motion picture, or more unusual choices that I just can't imagine. Memorializing your views will help you solidify them for yourself and will help others to gain insights from your experiences. You have learned how to create positive experiences in your life and others can certainly benefit from your experience.

2) Try to find other people who have a similar QOL and find out how much you have in common with them as well as how many ways in which you are different. Spread your viewpoint and philosophy to others who could most benefit from it. That is, to people who are somewhat disadvantaged for one reason or another. This might include young children, older adults, people who have a disability, or people who have a history of a mental health problem.

In summary, this chapter and the previous one presented information and recommendations for improving your QOL for each level of QOL. Recommendations given were unique for each level. They are meant to help you improve your QOL over the next 6 to 10 months. By using these recommendations and the recommendations in the previous chapter, you have a very good chance of improvement. The previous chapter focused especially on QOL scores that result from having more negative experiences in life than positive experiences. The current chapter focused on QOL scores that result from having more positive experiences than negative ones. In the previous chapter, improvements in QOL were based mainly upon reducing those negative experiences while secondarily increasing positive experiences. In the current chapter, the reverse was true. The focus was mostly on improving positive experiences and secondarily on reducing negative experiences. However, because everyone has some negative experiences, stressful events, and difficult times in their lives, the next chapter is devoted to obtaining a better understanding of stress and negative experiences and what to do about them. The purpose of the next chapter is to help you understand how distress comes about, ways to evaluate its seriousness, and what we know about coping with it. Avoiding, eliminating, or minimizing stress can help to make your QOL better. Remember, improving quality of life can occur in two ways. One way is to increase the number of positive experiences in your life, and the second way is to reduce the number of negative experiences in your life. A reduction in distress is still an improvement in quality of life.

COPING WITH NEGATIVE EXPERIENCES

CHAPTER 15: STRESS – A CONCEPTUAL MODEL

Figure 15.1

Conceptual Model of Stress and Coping

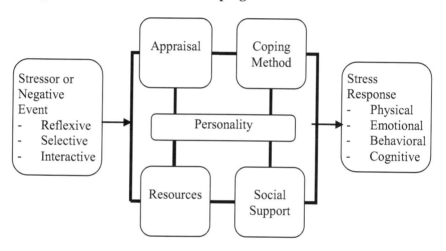

In the previous chapters, we focused a lot of attention on the role of positive experiences in promoting QOL. Now, we will turn our attention to negative experiences and their effects on QOL. Negative experiences may play a bigger role in determining overall QOL than do positive experiences. This is because many negative experiences last longer than positive experiences. Also, negative experiences generally have more of an emotional component than do positive experiences. For example, a study in the new field of behavioral economics showed that people have twice as much negative reaction to losing a certain amount of money in the stock market compared to positive experiences that come from gaining the same amount of money. Losing hurts more than winning excites.

In the previous chapters, we discussed three kinds of negative experiences: physical, psychological, and interpersonal. Their effects on QOL, however, can vary a great deal. There is no such thing as a life without negative experiences, and we all go through them from time to time over the course of life. In this chapter, we will discuss how these negative experiences come about and how they can be managed to make them as minimal as possible. We are not advocating that people take a "that didn't bother me" attitude toward the negative experiences in their lives, but rather how to minimize the damage they do and how to actually grow from them.

In our model of QOL, we have emphasized a **two-factor** approach. That is, there appears to be one broad factor accounting for high QOL. That broad factor is the number of positive **experiences** a person has and the kinds of **activities** that promote them. Low or negative QOL, on the other hand, is due to a high number of negative experiences caused by an entirely different set of events and activities. The accumulation of negative experiences is stressful. Specifically, a low QOL is caused by events that culminate in high levels of physical, emotional, and interpersonal distress. This chapter focuses more attention on the negative experiences and distressing side of the QOL scale. Negative experiences and distress arise from a general state we call "stress." Further, we will describe in detail what we mean by stress and distress, what we call stressors (the negative events in our lives that trigger stress), and the five major variables that intervene between stressors and stress to either minimize or exacerbate the stress response.

STRESS – A CONCEPTUAL MODEL
What do we mean by stress/distress?

Stress refers to the organized **physical response** of the body and the mind to a **perceived** threat. The body and mind is organized to help protect us in case of emergencies, urgent situations, and situations requiring immediate reactions. Stress is a complicated response or reaction that involves many separate systems in the body and, similarly, many processes in the brain and the mind. Distress is the emotional component of stress. It's the part that we feel psychologically. Stress/distress occurs in reaction to a stimulus, an event, or some kind of threat. The perceived threat can be to our physical body, or to our psychological well-being. Either one will evoke a stress response. We call these things stressors in order to distinguish them from the reaction they cause, which we call stress. We will go through each component of stress and the coping process as displayed in Figure 15.1. We will begin at the right hand side of the diagram by describing the stress response. We will describe stress in terms of our four components of experience: the physiological aspect, the emotional component, the behavioral component, and the cognitive component.

Physiologically, the stress response begins with the brain, because as far as we know now, it is the brain that perceives and interprets events as stressful or threatening or not. The brain constantly surveys our environment, and when it finds something that could potentially harm us, it sounds an alarm bell. The alarm bell triggers a response involving many systems below the brain. These systems include the muscles of the body, the autonomic nervous system, the endocrine system, and the immune system. The combined action of these systems creates what has been called the "fight or flight" syndrome. That is, they maximize the organism's systems to survive a serious, sometimes life threatening situation. Furthermore, this fight or flight reaction generally occurs automatically; thank goodness, we do not have to think about it. Once the brain sends out an alarm signal, the reaction takes over. Importantly, this reaction can also be started at the level below conscious awareness. Our brain may perceive a threat and respond to it even if we are not fully aware of what the threat is. For example, people suffering from panic disorders usually are not aware of what causes their extreme stress response. A panic attack is a full blown stress response. Physically, they would have started the pattern of organized responses in the fight or flight syndrome. That is, their heart rate would go up, their eyes would dilate, the blood vessels near the surface of the skin would constrict, glycogen would be released from the liver, blood pressure would increase, and other physical components would follow. Next, the system of glands in the body (endocrine system) would kick in to aid our survival. Especially important is the adrenal gland and its secretion of adrenalin. Adrenalin mimics the action of the autonomic nervous system and keeps the fight or flight response going longer and stronger. This and other hormones propel the body into "overdrive" by increasing muscle strength, decreasing a sense of pain, oxygenating the blood more, heightening our attention, and stopping non-essential bodily functions. This total physiological reaction occurs to help us deal with the potential harm that might be caused by a perceived threat. This stress response can vary from mild to severe depending upon how serious we perceive the threat to be.

When the fight or flight syndrome evolved in animals

millions of years ago, it was designed to be short-acting. That is, in just a few minutes, the animal or human either died, killed the predator, drove off the attacker, or fled from the attacker. Either way, it was all over in a relatively short period of time. The person or animal who survived returned to a state of relative calm and the stress response settled down. Today, the stressors and threats to our well-being are not usually short-term. Rather, they are likely to be long-term aggravations, frustrations, threats, disappointments, injuries, and other hardships that go on for a long time. Rather than having the stress response calm down after a short while, the stress response continues at a substantial level for a long period of time, even months and years. As a result, the very response of the body (such as increasing blood pressure, stopping digestion, tightening the muscle) can turn out to hurt us rather than to help us, because it can become continuous or chronic. The result may be conditions such as hypertension, fatigue, digestive problems, or headaches. Primary care physicians have estimated that 40% of the prescriptions they write are for stress related conditions, such as insomnia, anxiety, hypertension, depression, and pain. When either a diagnosable physical disorder or a diagnosable psychiatric disorder develops out of attempts to deal with high and/or prolonged stress, then a medical approach to reducing the stress (i.e., the use of medication) is a necessary but usually insufficient approach to improve it.

Finally, another physical response includes the action of muscle, because it is through muscles that we actually behave. When we perceive a threat, our muscles tense. They tense in order to prepare us for the fight or flight response. Muscles may increase their tension by one thousand percent compared to their resting state prior to the onset of stress. This tension usually goes unnoticed because we adapt to it and we do not recognize it as a problem until we develop pain, fatigue, or insomnia. Pain arises because the muscles either become exhausted or joints and ligaments are tightened more than usual. Fatigue arises because most of the energy that we derive from our food goes to our muscles. We consume the same amount of food that we normally do; however, under stress, our muscles might consume 20% more energy than they do when they are not stressed. During the day or by evening, we experience fatigue and tiredness setting in from prolonged muscle tension. Poor sleep is caused by tension, because sleep requires us to be relaxed. If we cannot relax, then muscle tension sends impulses up to the brain and keeps us awake. Very intensive training, usually of the biofeedback variety, is needed to help re-train the person to be aware of how much tension exists in the muscle. In my experience, people say they are relaxed at the beginning of treatment when the biofeedback machine says that they have moderate degrees of muscle tension. The person is unaware of the degree of tension because they have simply grown used to it and it is "normal" for them.

Stress also causes emotional reactions. These reactions depend upon how the person perceives the threats, the way they learned to deal with threats in the past, and similarity between previous threats and the current threats. The most common emotional reactions to threats are anger, fear, apathy, and depression. Rage is an intensified form of anger, and anxiety is a form of fear. All of these emotions are normal as long as they are proportional to the situations and are short lived. However, when these emotions are not proportional and go on for weeks or months, then they become a problem and an independent source of negative experience themselves. So now, there are two sources of negative experiences and we are heading for two more. The first one is the event that gave rise to the emotional reaction in the first place. That event has probably not been resolved. Otherwise the negative emotion would not keep going. The second negative experience is now the emotion itself, which is becoming a separate problem. It has by now triggered some portion of the physical stress response. Third, this prolonged emotion will negatively influence your interpersonal relationships, and that will add a further type of negative experience. Finally, if the emotional reaction goes on beyond a few weeks, then the chances of doing harm to yourself through a prolonged, low level, physiological stress response is very high. It is, therefore, important to address negative emotional states when they arise and not let them last more than a couple of weeks at most. It is important to understand that we have control over our stress reactions and to better understand how they arise.

We already said that one difference between stress today and stress tens of thousands of years ago is that, today, periods of stress last longer. Perhaps, though, the biggest difference between the cave man era and now is that in those days most of the threats were physical in nature. Dangerous animals, hazardous environments, and changing circumstances resulted in stress. Today, the largest source of stress is psychological in nature. Remember that the stress response starts when we **perceive** a threat to our physical or psychological well-being. By far the greatest source is psychosocial events. I seriously doubt that many of you have seen a saber-toothed tiger lately or been chased by a wooly mammoth. But I'll bet that most of you have had some kind of run in with another person, been disgruntled at work, found frustration with service you received somewhere, or wondered what someone meant by a certain remark. Today, our emotional reactions are much different. Even though there is nothing inherently stressful about these events, there is a great deal of variety in how people respond to these and similar events. The difference between the stress response and the thing that triggers it has led to referring to the latter as "stressor." That is, the event that triggers the response (i.e., the stressor) needs to be distinguished from the stress response itself. Surprisingly, the relationship between the nature and severity of the stressor and the magnitude and duration of the stress response is very low. In fact, research shows that the severity and frequency of a stressor accounts for only 20% to 25% of the emotional and physiological response to it. The other 75% to 80% of the stress response is due to variables intervening between the stimulus of the stressor and the stress response. That is, when we objectively measure characteristics of the stressor event, they don't turn out to be as important as we thought they would be. Instead, five critical psychological variables intervene between the objective stressor or event and the stress response. They either maximize or minimize the amount of stress that will occur. We will soon discuss these five variables. As an example, research on caregiver stress amongst spouses of people with Alzheimer's disease shows a very low relationship between the severity of the Alzheimer's disease plus the degree of help needed, and the stress of the caregiver/spouse. Instead, these other five variables account for most of the reasons for the stress or the absence of stress.

Stress also has a cognitive component. The cognitive component of stress affects more of **how** you think than **what** you think. Naturally, when a threat or potential harm is perceived, we have thoughts such as worry, retribution, and how to preserve our safety. However, the biggest effect is on our ability **to** think. When we perceive a minor threat to ourselves, such as a challenge or competition, our thinking may actually improve. When the threat is more severe and we perceive imminent or potential severe harm, our thinking ability becomes worse. Under normal circumstances, our thinking is characterized by being flexible, adaptive to new information, quick, able to recall past learning and knowledge, able to use information to make decisions, able to be aware of many things at one time, and able to problem solve. However, as one becomes more and more stressed, these abilities become more and more impaired. A highly stressed individual is not able to problem solve, shows stereotypical thinking, is illogical, is slow, cannot formulate the problem (let alone solve it), is not open to new information and interpretations, does not remember well, and shows poor judgment. Scores of studies in the psychological literature have demonstrated these points. In one study, rats were taught to jump from an elevated platform to one of two doors. One door was locked and behind the other door they were rewarded with food. If they bumped their noses on the closed door, they fell into a net and started over. When the platform was electrified and the animal was given a small shock, they performed well. However, when the rats were given a large shock, they performed poorly. When the experimenter locked the previous door that led to food and removed the previously locked door, the animals continued to jump to the newly locked door rather than jump through the now opened doorway to escape the shock. They did not go through the opened doorway until the experimenters picked them up and pushed them through the doorway. After the rats were shown the open doorway, they began to jump through the opened doorway on their own. This experiment shows many of the characteristics that people also display. Under high stress, people do not think of or try alternatives that might be available to them. Instead, they continue to try the same old things that have not worked in the past. Sometimes it takes another person to guide them to better alternatives. In the study just described, it is clear that it was high stress that caused stereotypical behavior. So here we have an example of how changes in emotional states (we can infer that it was stressful) can directly affect cognitive abilities through the mechanism of stress. People who are under stress are not usually aware of how illogical, automatic, and maladaptive their thinking becomes. You just have to imagine how bad this can be for a person suffering from major depression. The general stress is so high that he or she cannot think clearly and that is part of the diagnosis of the depression.

The behavioral component of stress includes your interpersonal behavior, your daily activities, and your behavioral expressions (e.g. facial expressions). When one perceives a threat to one's welfare, safety, or security, their interpersonal behavior shifts. In the simplest form, they either move toward people or away from people. If they move toward people, they do so either to seek support, solace, and protection, or to express anger or hostility. You might think of these two representing the behavioral expressions of fear and anger, respectively. The person who displays support-seeking behavior will adapt strategies and rules to help encourage this behavior from others. For example, a person such as this might be expected to exaggerate consciously or unconsciously physical symptoms as a way of asking for help. On the other hand, another person may express behavioral aspects of anger and go after what they perceive to be the source of their torment and potential harm. Under high stress, these people may verbally or even physically attack others, whether it is justified or not. For example, a person may believe it is his boss's fault that he got fired rather than his own incompetence. He may, in turn, express his anger toward the boss by verbally or physically attacking him. At the extreme, it is sometimes called "going postal". People who move away from other people during a time of stress are more likely to express apathetic or depressive emotional states of stress through their behaviors. These people reduce the number of contacts they usually have, isolate themselves at home, tend to increase their consumption of alcohol, and do not bring their problems to others who may be able to assist.

The behavioral aspect of the stress response also includes its effect on daily activities. As you might guess, pleasurable, successful, and meaningful activities decrease by approximately 50% in people with severe stress. In one study conducted by my colleagues and I, people who were clinically depressed were evaluated on the number of these activities in which they engaged during the previous week. They were found to have between 40% and 50% fewer such activities than age-matched, non-depressed individuals. After they were successfully treated for depression, and throughout the course of the treatment, the number of such positive activities gradually increased for them. At the end of six months of treatment, not only had depression disappeared as a problem for most people, but the number of positive activities they participated in was then the same as the comparison group. This example demonstrates the fact that the behavioral aspect of the overall stress response is very powerful and must be addressed in order for us to reduce negative experiences and increase positive experiences.

This section has described the stress response. We emphasized four main components of the response, including physiological, emotional, cognitive, and behavioral. Negative experiences are either a partial stress response (such as a negative emotion) or a full stress response (physiological, emotional, cognitive, and behavioral reactions) whether the person experiences it as such or not. Our purpose has been to lay the ground work for how stress and other negative experiences can be reduced in order to improve one's QOL. Remember, improving QOL means reducing negative experiences as well as increasing positive experiences. If you imagine stress to be on a 10 point-scale, if you can keep your stress level around 2 to 3 with an occasional increase of up to 6 or even 7, you are doing well. However, if you find your level of stress is consistently around 6 or higher, that's a problem. Physical and psychiatric disorders begin to emerge when a person's stress level is around 7 or 8 for more than two or three months. Next, we will describe the nature of stressors and then turn our attention to the five variables that lie between stressors and stress that can help to minimize excess stress.

CHAPTER 16: THREE TYPES OF STRESSORS

What do we mean by "stressor"?

The word "stressor" may be new to you. Most people have heard the term stress but few of them have heard the term "stressor." The reason we need this term is that "stress" refers to the **response** animals and humans have to a perceived threat. We need a term that describes those threats. That is, if stress is a response, what is it a response to? Many people make the mistake of saying or implying that the stress is something outside of them, such as "I have a stressful job" or "I have a stressful friendship". It is sometimes difficult with this language to know which is the cause and which is the effect. It even gets more muddled, such as an expression of "You make me mad." Actually, the last sentence is psychologically impossible. In truth, someone does something and someone else gets mad, but there is no one-to-one connection between the two. Therefore, we try to separate stressors from stress.

There are many taxonomies for characterizing stressors. For the purpose of this book, I am going to take the route of dividing them into just three classes. The first class we will label **reflexive**. This refers to the class of stressors that are more or less wired in and cause everyone to have a stress response in relation to them. In other words, the stress response is almost entirely caused by the nature of the stressor and nearly everyone reacts the same way. These are mostly life threatening events or stressors. These stressors were present even during the days of the Neanderthal. They are strongly related to survival. These stressors include earthquakes, fire, tsunamis, pain, extreme hunger, extreme thirst, near death experiences, predators, falling from a substantial height, death of a cherished offspring, and severe weather. Nearly everyone today is capable of being stressed by these things. However, these stressors account for less than 10% of the average person's stressors during a year.

Next, there is a class of stressor which we call **selective**. These are stressors unique to a few individuals and are restricted to several actual objective events. Stressors such as these are the ones related to phobic reactions, panic attacks, or post-traumatic stress reactions that some people experience. These stressors include snakes, spiders, elevators, heights, airplanes, germs, certain colors, isolation, painful memories, or stimuli that are similar - objectively or symbolically - to an original traumatic event. In these cases, the stress response is mostly determined by the nature of the stressor, but it is also influenced by the five factors described below. The unique thing about these stressors is they cause extreme stress in the selective few people they affect. These may also account for about 10% of all stressors during a year.

The last class of stressors we will call **interactive**. We call these interactive because the external stressors interact with five critical internal factors under our control to create the ultimate degree, type, and duration of the stress response. We will discuss these five factors shortly. This class is the most important one for our understanding of modern day stress. Most of them are due to living in cities with socio-cultural customs and more. There is great variability in people's reactions to these objective events because internal factors vary so much person to person. These kinds of stressors account for about 80% to 90% of a person's yearly stress and negative experiences. Most people would find these events somewhat stressful, but the stress response could range from very mild to very severe depending upon those other five factors. The objective event itself (such as heavy traffic or a quarrel with someone) accounts for only about 25% of these stress responses. The other 70% to 80% is due to the other five factors to be discussed and the interaction between those factors and the objective event.

Examples of interactive stressors include heavy traffic, getting into an argument with a loved one, being criticized by a superior, giving a speech before a group, the death of a relative, onset of disability, moving, not having enough money to meet expenses, moderate to severe pain, rejection by others, and auto accidents. Research shows, for example, that there is little relationship between the severity of a patient's dementia and the level of the caregiver's stress. The stress caregivers feel comes mostly from those other five factors. To put it in abstract terms, consider the events that trigger stress to be represented by the color yellow. Now consider the five variables internal to you (to be discussed next) to be represented by the color red. What you respond to with your stress response is neither to the yellow nor to the red but to orange, the mixture of the events and your own make up. The good news or the bad news, depending on how you look at it, is that you control at least 60% of your own negative experiences and stress. The good news about this is that you can therefore bring your own negative experiences and stress under your own greater control. The bad news is you really can't blame others for your experiences.

The person who is not handling stress very well will have the maximum amount of negative experiences as a result. First, they tend to look at a stressor as though it were a reflexive or selective stressor. They believe their response is entirely due to an objective event instead of realizing that **they** are participants in creating their own stress. They blame their physical, emotional, and behavioral responses on the event and declare that anyone would feel the same way. In fact, other people don't feel the same way. There is great variability in responses to most objective events. Furthermore, people do have substantial control over their stress responses, as evidenced by this large variability. The person who is highly stressed also does not recognize the **five factors** that lie between the triggering event and their stress response. On the contrary, people who have the least amount of stress possible, given the situation, do recognize these factors. They realize that they are mostly under their own control and use them positively. Last, the person who is maximally stressed "spreads" the stress to a larger circle, making even more negative experiences for himself or herself. In addition to the original triggering event, such as pain, their poor coping leads to friction with other people because they will emotionally strike out at others with anger or rage, or may become hopelessly dependent on others and not shoulder sufficient self responsibility. This spread may continue further, so that eventually a person like this could end up with the stress of a divorce or the stress of being abandoned. This occurs because he or she had a poor time coping with the initial interactive stressor. This spreading effect is sometimes referred to as a "cascade of disasters."

THREE TYPES OF STRESSORS

Five factors that can reduce your stress and increase your control

One thing highly stressed people have in common is that they don't feel that they have much control over events or their responses to events. People feel like they are dealing with reflective stressors instead of with interactive stressors. Undoubtedly though, the vast majority of stressors are the interactive kind, where the triggering event kicks off a series of other events that eventually determine the ultimate stress response. Keeping a stress response to as minimal a level as possible will also prevent other negative experiences, such as the onset of psychological disorders, the onset of illnesses and accidents, interpersonal problems with people who are needed, and various symptoms such as insomnia, digestive problems, and fatigue. Please refer to Figure 15.1. There you will find the five factors that are displayed between stressors on the left and the stress responses on the right. These five factors can eliminate, minimize, or, if wrongly used, maximize the amount of stress a person experiences from a given stressor. We will address these factors one at a time.

Personality

The most unifying factor is your personality. Your personality can draw you into the stressful situations in the first place or keep you out of stressful situations. Your personality characteristics can also help you cope with stressors or impede your ability to cope with stressors. Your personality may also allow you to seek assistance for difficulties or may make it difficult for you to seek assistance. These three dynamics – exposure to stressful situations, coping with them, and seeking assistance for them – are influenced in great amount by your personality characteristics. For example, if you find yourself having the same old kinds of arguments with your spouse and you end up feeling frustrated, make sure your personality isn't preventing you from approaching the disagreements in a different and more productive nature. You may be the kind that likes to win a technical point with someone else, but you lose the affection of the other person in the process. There is a strong relationship between personality factors and the number and kinds of stressors (therefore the number of negative experiences) a person has. If you have stressors that continue beyond eight weeks or so, and you are not able to reduce or eliminate them by simple means, such as described below, then we have to look further for an explanation. One possibility is that there is something about your personality that draws you into a situation that becomes stressful, or there is something about your personality that prevents you from withdrawing from a stress-producing situation. It may be one of the five personality traits described in Chapter 12. If you recall, in Chapter 12 you were asked to rate yourself on five personality traits. Review those results for a minute, and think of them in the context of being one of the factors mediating between stressors and stress. Also notice that in the diagram in Figure 15.1, personality is centered among four other variables that are important in their own right but are also connected to your personality and connected to each other. This diagram illustrates that, for example, a person with a low level of motivation (a personality trait) would likely choose a different kind of coping method than someone with higher motivation. Someone who has lower motivation is inclined to pick a method that reduces stress quickly, even if, in the long run, it is not helpful. Your personality traits can likewise influence how much support you will receive from others, what kind of resources you will gather and use, and how you will appraise your current situation and your own abilities. Thus if any of the personality traits listed in Chapter 12 were scored by you as being in the "not like me" category, this could add substantially to your stress one way or another. Any shift to the left will improve the way you handle stress and negative experiences considerably.

Appraisal

This term, appraisal, has come to mean how people view their circumstances, including their current situation, their own ability to deal with things, and the future. People have an amazing ability to view the same situation in suprisingly different ways. The way that they view their situation and themselves is a stronger predictor of their degree of stress than any objective characteristic of the stressor. The most important appraisal that a person makes in terms of the stress model is how much potential threat and harm they see in the stressor. For example, two different people sitting in their cars in the same heavy freeway traffic may have two entirely different viewpoints about it. One might say to himself, "This traffic is terrible. I am wasting my time on the freeway. Why did I take a job so far from home? I must be an idiot. I might get killed on this freeway one day." He grips his steering wheel, grits his teeth, and notices he has a headache. His stress is high, and it's mostly due to his appraisal (his self talk) about the situation and himself. He has a drink when he arrives home, but this only makes him more irritable and he has an argument with his wife. The other driver, sitting in the next lane, also is in the same traffic. He says to himself, "I don't much care for the traffic, but it does give me time to catch up on that latest book I have been listening to on the CD. I'll call ahead with my voice activated phone and tell my wife I will be late. I will just enjoy this book until I get home. I'm glad that I planned ahead for such an occasion." He will have much less stress (but not an absence of stress), and he will arrive home more relaxed compared to the other driver. His appraisal of the situation, and his response to it, has helped him minimize his stress. His personality is open to new experiences, including ones he doesn't expect. When they come along, he is better equipped to produce more positive appraisals of the situation than negative ones. Our customary appraisals of situations and ourselves often go on at an unconscious level. We don't know how we think because it is the way we have always thought. Negative appraisals are usually automatic and instantaneous, illogical and negative, but it usually takes someone else to point those characteristics out.

Social Support

Social support refers to both instrumental and emotional support that individuals receive from others. Instrumental support means help with everyday activities, such as shopping, cooking, house cleaning, taking someone to the doctor, etc. Emotional support means providing encouragement, a soft shoulder, caring, and understanding to another. People who are under stress want and need more support, and the more stress they experience, the more support they want and need. Support comes from either informal sources, such as family and friends, or from formal sources, such as doctors and therapists.

Thousands of research studies have found that receiving support, and the right kind of support at the right time, reduces our stress significantly. Part of this reduction in stress is due to being reassured that others are willing and capable of helping. This heightens a sense of safety and security. So, for example, studies showed that during the acute phases of serious illness, doctors, nurses, and therapists are rated as being the most important sources of support. But when the patient returns home, families and friends are rated as being the most important source of support. Garnering, keeping, and balancing support from others, with contributions given back to others, is an important step in dealing with stress on a long-term basis. People do not generally need an inordinate amount of support, but they do need enough support to deal with both their emotional support needs and their instrumental support needs. The person who is stressed also has to bear the majority of responsibility in creating and maintaining their support system. As part of this, three rules are to be followed: 1) you cannot expect somebody else to create social support systems for you; 2) you cannot be so irritable, crabby, or unappreciative that you drive others away; and 3) the personality trait of seeking assistance should be in the positive range so that you will allow others to help support you (Chapter 12).

For example, if I need such a support system, and I am willing to seek assistance for myself, I would make sure I have a primary care doctor that I can see regularly. Additionally, I would keep or try to identify two or three close friends who I could use as confidants and that I can use for emotional support (including my wife). And I would line up and get as much help as I need for my instrumental support, preferably not having the same people that I have for my emotional support.

Coping Method

An additional factor that is very important in determining the ultimate level of stress is the method or methods that a person adopts to cope with the perceived stressor. There is a wide variety of methods people can use to cope, some of which are better and some of which are worse. We can group some of these together and note that there are basically four kinds: two that are not helpful and two that are helpful. One of the unhelpful methods is to become what is called "emotion-focused." That is, the person primarily expresses his stress through his emotions - whether it is irritability, panic, depression, frustration, or another emotion. Plus, they let everyone around them know how bad they feel emotionally. They will tell anyone who will listen to their story of misery and how they feel emotionally as a result. They seek sympathy, support, and agreement from others, but only if they agree with these other people. People who use this coping method primarily are also attempting to avoid blame or responsibility for their situation. Not understanding or not being able to express all the aspects of stress, it goes on and on.

The second not-so-helpful method is self-destructive. Under normal times, these people function fairly well, but when a major stressor occurs they are very likely to use drugs, excess alcohol, sex, or illegal acts to express how they feel or distract them from it. Both of these not-so-helpful methods lead to further negative consequences, which just enlarge the circle of stress and continued use of the unhelpful coping methods.

One of the two helpful coping methods is what we call "problem-focused". These people recognize that they have a problem and try to solve it. For example, if they have marital difficulties, they would seek out counselors. If a child is failing in school, they will seek an assessment of the child. If there is not enough money to get through the next few months, the problem-solving person will prioritize their needs. They display an appropriate emotional reaction, but at the same time begin to formulate a plan of action to solve the problem. These people keep stress to a level no higher than it needs to be. By contrast, the emotion-focused coper will focus on the emotion rather than the underlying problem.

Last, there is a powerful method of coping that requires courage and taking responsibility for oneself. This involves taking responsibility for having caused the stress, and working backwards to see how you did it to yourself. Looking backward would include seeing how you got involved in the stressful situation in the first place, and going through each of the five intervening variables (coping, personality, etc.) to determine how you ended up at this degree of stress. This approach will not only help you gain insight, but taking responsibility will help you to see what you need the most to improve your situation. There is only about 20% of the population, in my experience, who are capable of using this kind of approach to dealing with their stress in life. However, even they will be the first ones to tell you that, after identifying all of the contributors to their own stress, they still need assistance of various forms in dealing with it. The most favorable outcomes from this approach to coping with stress are that it strengthens the person's abilities for dealing with future stress and it reduces current stress to a more manageable level.

Resources

The last factor in our model is resources. By this we mean the monetary, informational, friendship, business, property, and personal resources you can bring to bear to help deal with stressful situations. Naturally, if money is not an object, you can mostly get whatever you need. But let's be realistic; money *is* an object. Most people do not have extra funds available to use as they wish. This still leaves a lot of other resources to help solve problems that would, in turn, reduce stress. These other resources include friends and neighbors, information that you can get online, churches, nonprofit organizations, business associations, and governmental agencies. Let us give you an example. Someone in our family needed a safety bar installed in front of a bathtub. He did not want to risk slipping and falling into the tub and injuring himself. It was hard to find information about such a bar. He called his brother, and in the course of conversation, he described what he was looking for. His brother said, "I know exactly what you need, and I have it right here in my garage. It is a self-expanding bar that was made to go between two loads on a truck in order to keep the loads separated. But it can be used between two walls and you will have a very secure bar." Voila! The problem was solved. No cost and easily done. We all have access to information from other people and from professionals who can serve as resources to us. For example, I have cultivated a good relationship with my doctor. I trust him and he trusts me. I can call him on the phone, and he will call me back. He makes suggestions about my medicine and will order new prescriptions for me, and I tell him how I am doing. I have found that whenever I bring up the topic of resources with patients or clients, they only think of money as a resource until we start going through other categories of resources. Even if they don't have computers, they can go to just about any public library, community college, university, community center, or senior center, and use one free of charge.

This chapter highlighted two major points concerning negative experiences and stress. The first point was that there are three kinds of stressors, with the far more common and consequential called interactive stressors. These stressors are a result of the event or events that seemingly started the stress, but have a major contribution from five other variables that interact with these original events to ultimately be the causes of the stress and the degree of stress. The second major point was that these five interactive and intervening variables play powerful roles in helping us to manage or avoid negative experiences. The more realistically we can appraise events, use our existing resources, develop support, and cope with those events, the more we will be able to reduce the negative experiences in our lives that contribute to our stress. It is not possible to go through life stress-free. However, we can achieve ways of managing stress that reduce it from overwhelmingly negative and noxious levels to something more manageable and even something that will be beneficial in terms of learning ways of better coping for the future.

CHAPTER 17: REDUCING STRESS AND NEGATIVE EXPERIENCES

Given the discussion above on the nature of stress and its causes, it follows that there are several techniques for reducing stress and negative experiences. The first thing we need to know is, how stressed are you? This question is not very easy to answer because many of the symptoms of stress are physiological, such as our blood pressure, and not within our conscious awareness. Also, some levels of high psychological stress may be taken as "normal" by a person because they do not have adequate comparisons or because they have learned to live with fairly high levels of stress and consider it normal. It is difficult for a person to know how stressed they should be when the death of a loved one occurs. I have often been asked by patients, "Should I still be this upset four weeks after my relative died?" Having no comparisons to make and not knowing what to expect, people are confused by the process of grief and need some external expertise to tell them whether they are feeling normal or not. Likewise, a man who has been coping for three years with a wife who has debilitating Alzheimer's disease may not recognize how gradually he has slipped into a state of major depression because now it feels "normal." Given that people often are not able to identify their own degree of stress, we are left with three key indicators of stress: physical findings as discovered by your doctor, psychological findings as discovered by a licensed professional, and your own self report or self assessment. In terms of self assessment, if you think of the stress response physically and psychologically and interpersonally on a 10 point scale, then stress at a level of 7 or higher that goes on for four weeks or longer needs to be addressed. Naturally we want to have people aim to have stress levels not higher than 2 on a 10 point scale, with occasional episodes of 5 or 6 or 7. However, we want to avoid long-lasting levels that are moderately high and acute levels that are exceedingly high (9 or 10). The former are damaging, both physically and psychologically, and the latter are acute emergencies and may lead to severe disturbance or death. The starting place for determining what techniques to emphasize in dealing with stress is to determine how stressed you currently are. Based upon our previous discussion, you can see that we can begin by directing our attention to one or more of three places. We can reduce the stress response directly if we need to, we can try to adjust the objective stressor event somehow, or we can try to adjust the 5 intervening variables. Let me give you examples of each. When all indicators show that the stress response is very high and that it is doing damage physically or psychologically, then we need to consider addressing the stress response itself directly. When stress results in a diagnosable disorder, whether physical or psychological (such as hypertension or major depression), then it should be attacked aggressively. This will almost always include the use of a medication because that is the quickest and surest way to get the most severe symptoms under control. If we do not get severe symptoms under control quickly, there is a high probability that the person will have a major medical event or be too psychiatrically disabled to apply most other treatments. Eventually, with proper medicine, the stress- related symptoms will improve. However, nothing has been done to alter the triggering event, or the person's way of coping. Medication will almost certainly work, but it will come at a cost of having to stay on the medicine and not learning better ways to deal with stress.

The second general approach is to do something about the triggering events that we call stressors. This would involve staying away from the identified stressor and any others like it, reducing the frequencies of exposure to it, or getting rid of the perceived stressor. For example, if a person is in an abusive relationship, then something should be done about helping the person remove himself or herself from that situation. Removing oneself from truly dangerous or damaging situations is vital. However, removing oneself from situations that are not dangerous, but rather are annoying or anxiety-provoking only, is probably not the right solution. While this method may work, it also comes at a high cost. People may begin to learn to avoid too many situations because they cannot cope with the anxiety that comes with them. As a result, people may also be giving up situations that also provide positive experiences, and this further reduces their quality of life. For example, if a person avoids flying, they may lose the opportunity to go on pleasant trips with others.

Finally, there are the five intervening variables that we can focus on to help reduce the stress. Focusing on the five intervening variables (personality, appraisal, social support, coping method, and resources) is important because they account for more than 60% of the stress we experience and because they are the factors that we can most easily learn to control and change. Remember our two drivers on the freeway? They are exposed to the same event. However, one driver processed the event differently than the other driver and shaped the event into a less negative experience, if not even a positive experience. One event, two different experiences. This happened because these five intervening variables always are present and play a major role in whether we experience a severely negative event, a somewhat negative event, or even a positive event. Naturally, the best way to proceed in managing stress and reducing negative experiences is to combine all three approaches and to use the right methods at the right time to deal with the negative events in life.

CHAPTER 18: SEVEN SPECIFIC WAYS TO MANAGE STRESS AND NEGATIVE EXPERIENCES

1: Reducing the Physical and Psychological Stress Directly

Sometimes stress can reach such high levels that it produces a physical or psychological change that can actually be diagnosed. These physical or psychological disorders, such as hypertension or depression, mean that the stress has taken on a life of its own and exists in a form that is hurting us above and beyond the original events that brought it on. Stress from too many work demands or too little money is stressful in itself, but when this stress is continued for a long time and at high levels, it often takes the form of one of these diagnosable disorders and then that disorder itself represents a major problem. Thus stress at work may cause high blood pressure, but should the high blood pressure continue at high levels and for too long, it may cause a stroke, which is an entirely different problem and source of more stress. When stress reaches such levels, sometimes the most important approach is to directly treat the stress-related physical or psychological problem that has been created. Unless, and until, we can get these stress-related problems under better control, other approaches at improving the management of stress and reducing negative events will not work as well. Usually this requires medical assistance to help reduce severe stress symptoms. Medicines are the surest and quickest way to reduce stress-related illnesses. The appropriate use of medications is for a diagnosable disorder. Although many people may frown on taking medicines, they are truly a miracle of the 20th and 21st centuries. Where would we be without medicines that reduce blood pressure, decrease pain, or treat depression? Millions of lives have been shortened and made unbearable over the many decades and centuries before the advent of these medicines. Medicines will help to diminish the negative experiences as well as to help reduce the physical symptoms. Only a licensed professional can determine whether the amount and kind of stress you are experiencing would benefit from a medicine. We neither want to give medicine to people who don't need it, nor do we want to withhold it from people who would truly benefit from it. The secret to using medications the proper way is to seek an evaluation from a physician, psychiatrist, psychologist, or other licensed health professional who can help to determine whether medication would be helpful. Too often, people self-medicate to reduce the distressing psychological symptoms of stress or they do the opposite and resist or ignore the benefits that may be derived from an appropriate evaluation. If you or a loved one believe that your stress has gone on too long or has caused a change in the way you usually function or relate to others then, by all means, you should seek an evaluation for yourself. Today's medications are very safe compared to 20 years ago and are very effective at reducing levels of stress to where other techniques will be of benefit also.

If your stress does not result in a diagnosable disorder according to your doctor or health care provider, there are still several techniques that can directly reduce the physical and psychological stress itself. Methods for directly reducing physical and psychological symptoms of stress that can be used by themselves or in conjunction with medications, depending upon the degree of stress, include biofeedback, acupuncture, yoga, meditation, exercise, nutrition, hypnosis, or counseling. Biofeedback is a method wherein some measure of the person's "biology," such as their heart rate, muscle tension, or sweating, is fed back to them using some identifiable signal. It has been shown that by providing feedback to a person about their own response, he or she can gain control over it and greatly reduce their stress. My favorite form of biofeedback was using a measure of muscle tension to feed back to the person how tense he or she was. People who thought they were calm and relaxed could be shown that, in fact, they were generating very high levels of muscle tension. By teaching the person to recognize and control the level of their muscle tension, it was possible over a matter of about 12 to 15 sessions to greatly reduce the level of stress and teach the person how to control it even in the absence of the equipment we originally used for training. I have found acupuncture, the insertion of very fine needles into selected spots in the body, to be of benefit especially for the treatment of pain. Pain is a very complex response in the body, triggered and exacerbated by many different physical and psychological processes. We do not have a thorough understanding of all of the mechanisms involved in pain so there is room for many approaches. Acupuncture is based upon eastern approaches to curing that identify and stimulate energy centers throughout the body. People report that acupuncture can reduce pain from anywhere around 10% to a 90% reduction. In addition, acupuncture can be used for general anxiety and for reducing symptoms such as irritable bowel syndrome. Several forms of yoga exist that focus on different aspects of religious philosophies and which teach the person to gain greater control over their internal processes, such as breathing, "energy flow," awareness of their body, and mental imagery. Meditation is not the same as yoga. Meditation is a way of focusing attention by concentrating on a single process, such as breathing, or on a mental image. Meditation is meant to relax the body and bring it into "harmony" with its surroundings or else to insulate it from harsh surroundings. Meditation is a useful technique for anyone to learn and may reduce general stress levels by as much as 50%. Exercise is a powerful technique for reducing stress for three different reasons. First, exercise burns off excessive hormones in the body that could otherwise do damage if they were not metabolized. This is particularly true in the case of cortisol, which is known to be high in people undergoing excessive levels of stress. Second, exercise builds strength and endurance, which are helpful in fighting off stress and for keeping it to lower levels. Third, exercise is important because it produces self confidence in people who continue it and who are able to achieve goals as they progress through an exercise program. People benefit from all three products of a good 30-minute-per-day exercise program. Proper nutrition is an essential part of managing stress. Under times of stress, we tend to eat food that is readily available, cheap, and that gives us an immediate relief from the stress. The top six nutrients in this class are sugar, sugar, sugar, caffeine, fats, and simple carbohydrates. When we eat those things, they rapidly digest, give us a burst of energy, and then rapidly deplete themselves. People who eat this way usually end up feeling exhausted so they have to repeat the process throughout the day. However, every time they repeat the process, it becomes worse and they have few true nutritional ingredients left in their system for managing the physical demands of

...ss. A program of proper nutrition greatly aids combating stress. It should include about 20% protein, about 65% complex carbohydrates, about 10% simple carbohydrates, and 5% healthy oils. This balance will provide immediate energy and energy that lasts throughout a seven or eight hour period. Then it's time to eat again. Finally, hypnosis is a powerful tool for managing stress when it is provided by a licensed physician, dentist, or psychologist. Hypnosis, contrary to stereotypes about it, does not produce a state of unconscious. Instead, it increases a person's awareness of things going on in and around them. Under the right circumstances, hypnosis can be used for any stress-related disorder including overeating, general anxiety, exhaustion, and low to moderate depression. The main ingredients in successful hypnosis are a trusting relationship with the therapist and an ability to focus one's attention on various topics. All these methods, from medication to hypnosis, can directly treat the stress response itself, depending upon the level and severity of that response. We now turn our attention to several other techniques that can treat the complex ingredients involved in the development and continuation of stress.

2: Avoiding or Reducing the Frequency of Triggering Events

Second, we can address the stressor itself. Most stressors will be of the interactive type, so it is difficult to talk about the stressors separately from the five interactive factors that affect them, but we will try. You can think of these stressors as the triggering event and the five other variables as those which elaborate on the triggering event. One thing that might be possible is to avoid a particular stressor altogether. If heavy traffic on the way to work is a major stressor for

178

you, maybe you can change your work schedule to avoid heavy u.. Maybe you can go in early and come home early. Maybe you can carpool with others and make it less stressful. If you cannot avoid it altogether, maybe you can reduce its frequency. If you can't go to work early and go home early every day, maybe you can do it two days a week. If you notice that your spouse gets upset every time you bring up a certain topic, stop bringing up the topic. Or, if you find that doing household chores is stressful for you, you may find it helpful to pay somebody else to do it. While we believe that it is the elaborating five variables that are more important than the triggering event itself in causing stress, it is nevertheless important to consider avoiding the stressful event altogether. This would be especially important in the case of highly dangerous events, such as abusive relationships or illegal activities. Sometimes it is best to just stay away. But because stressors interact with those other five variables we discussed, we also have to show how those factors can change a stressor. Earlier in this book we described those five factors. To refresh your memory, these are how we view or appraise the event, how we presently cope with those events, the support that we receive from others, the resources we have available, and our own personality. We will share some techniques on how to change them in the next sections.

3: Tweaking Your Personality

Our personality is important in relationship to stress in two significant ways. First, once a triggering event occurs (such as dense traffic), it will evoke our long-standing habits of dealing with such events. These long-standing habits can be thought of as your

179

personality. They are the ways you consistently respond to threatening or potentially harmful situations. If you are consistently optimistic, you may think, "Well, the traffic will probably lighten up soon." If you are consistently pessimistic you might think, "Well, what is going to happen to me next?" These long term habits are really more important than the event itself in determining your stress. The second way personality is important is that it may account for why you are drawn into certain situations and events to begin with. Why do some people choose to hang out with the wrong people or engage in dangerous activities? What about their personalities lead them to make these choices in the first place? If we could change these people's personalities just a little, what we mean by tweaking it, we could get a dramatic decrease in the amount of stress they experience or the frequency of stress they experience. Either one would be an improvement. It is not necessary to conduct a full change of personality, even if we wanted to. Instead, it has been my experience that many people will change their personality spontaneously if they simply know what part of it is the problem. This is where either expert opinion or the use of psychological questionnaires may come in handy. If a person is told by an "authority" that they are too pessimistic or can see it for themselves in the results of questionnaires, particularly if the results are based on valid observations, a person may learn to recognize that they are being a little too pessimistic and stop a chain reaction of other negative thoughts and behaviors.

We can start by examining your personality profile from Chapter 12. Let's make sure you are not contributing a major portion to your own stress and negative experiences because of your own personality. Scores to the right hand side of the midpoint probably have an effect on your negative experiences and therefore on your QOL. As we go through subsequent sections, we will discuss how these personality traits can interact with other factors in turning a low stress situation into a high stress situation or vice versa. For now, you should pay particular attention to those personality traits that you endorsed as being "not like me" or "mostly not like me." Your goal should be to bring them more to the centerline or even the plus side on the left. The reason for this suggestion is that scores to the right of the center probably indicate that you have difficulties viewing events realistically, interacting with other people, and coping with stress. For example, if your score on the trait of believing you have control over events in your life is either "not like me" or "mostly not like me," then you probably believe your life is under control by others or random events. You are underestimating your ability to be in charge of your life and to determine both the kinds of experiences you will have and your overall QOL. It is difficult, in the confines of this book, to fully describe how to change any of these personality traits. However, all irrational personality traits have their basis in unsupported beliefs that you have about yourself, limited experience, and automatic thinking (that is, springing to a conclusion without examining the evidence). These traits can be modified. Probably the easiest method is to talk over your results with your life partner, with a close friend, or with a professional counselor, to help determine the origin of these traits and why they are sustained.

4: Appraisal, Viewpoint, and Attitude

Fourth, changing your customary method of appraisal will

require you to share your viewpoints with somebody else and to be open to feedback from them. If you have unrealistic or maladaptive appraisals, either will show up in the language you use. Maladaptive appraisals are usually characterized by the use of extreme words. These include words such as: failure, stupid, worthless; or words that set limits on possibilities such as: have to, must, must not, should, could not, etc. Most maladaptive appraisals are illogical and unsupported by evidence. For further assistance in being able to change your appraisal, there are suggested readings at the end of the book. Recall the example we gave of two people driving in the same traffic earlier in this chapter. That example was meant to show how the stressor itself is changed by the person's appraisal. This action of appraising how much threat, harm, or frustration may rise in a stressor is sometimes referred to as "framing." A powerful technique for reducing the impact of a stressor is to **reframe** how it is viewed. For example, a student who fails a midterm examination and says to himself, "I'm so stupid. I failed everything." is a person who is going to have a high amount of stress. On the other hand, a person, in response to the same failed midterm, might frame his viewpoint as "Boy, I sure blew that exam. I guess I didn't give enough study time. Next time, I am going to at least triple the amount of time I am studying for it." This person will have much less stress. The degree of threat or potential harm in any event or activity is determined by how it is perceived. Perception of the event or activity is also a part of the appraisal process. I imagine that neither God nor Superman perceived much threat in any event. As mentioned, the appraisal process is very powerful. It takes less than a quarter of a second for a person to size up the situation and make some internal appraisals about it. Research has shown that appraisal of an event accounts for more of the stress response than the actual event itself. In other words, things are what you make of them.

5: Coping Techniques

The fifth technique has to do with specific coping techniques that you use. When faced with threat, we all use different methods to try to reduce the threat. We call these methods coping methods, or coping styles. Sometimes these are called defense mechanisms when they apply to psychological threats. Earlier, we described four coping styles or methods, two positives and two negatives. The best technique in this regard for managing stress and negative experiences is to make sure that you are not using negative styles. You should instead be using positive styles. Negative styles include using such maladaptive behaviors as: denying the problem, using mind-altering substances to blunt the experience, blaming others, driving too fast, rationalizing your behavior, or excessive spending. Instead, you can use more adaptive techniques, such as those described earlier (e.g., problem solving, developing new skills, seeking advice). These would include taking responsibility for your contribution to the stress, and sharing your expressions and your situation with others who may be able to help. In other words, stop using that which doesn't work and start using that which does work.

6: Optimizing Social Support

Sixth, the judicious use of social support during times of stress is very important. It's especially important when little can be done to change the event that triggers the stress, and sometimes the only way to deal with it is to go through it. For example, the death of a loved one will be very stressful to anyone. You cannot change what happened, and the person needs to go through normal grieving, even though it is stressful. Social support at a time like this is critical. The best technique is to use social support as a buffer between life's negative events. It is in your best interest to already have at least a small network of friends and family in place, and be willing to use them when necessary. Here we can see an example how this variable, social support, interacts with one's personality. If a person scored on the right-hand side regarding the trait of seeking assistance, then they probably won't ask for help and won't allow others who volunteer to help them. This will cut off a major factor in dealing with stress. On the other hand, research shows that people who allow themselves to be supported through times of trouble do much better in the long run.

7: Knowing Your Resources

Finally, we come to the variable of resources. Remember, this doesn't include just money. It includes other people, information, organizations, benefits, and institutions that could be helpful to you. Improving or knowing the resources that are available can help you to feel less alone and feel more powerful in the face of stress. A good technique to follow is to catalog all of your resources. Think about and write down all of the specific resources you have under these categories and other categories you may think of. Picture scenarios that could happen to you in your life and ask yourself what resources you could turn to for specific kinds of problems. You will find out quickly where you stand and what kind of resources you need to cultivate for yourself, not only for the stressful situation you are experiencing now. For example, who and what would you turn to if your house were to burn down? Where would you live? How would you keep up a normal life? Who and what would you turn to if you suffered a severe injury? How could you work? Who would help you with dressing and bathing? How would you get around? Who and what would you turn to if you lost your job? How would you support yourself? Who would you turn to for help? Preparing for scenarios such as these will help you realize what resources you have, and what resources you need. It may also provide you with more confidence in your ability to manage stressors.

If you utilize the methods and techniques described in this chapter, you can minimize the impact of potential stress-producing events. You can learn to shorten the duration of negative experiences. In turn, you can improve your QOL by spending less time and energy on negative events and spending more time on positive events.

Case Example

It might be a good idea at this point to demonstrate how all of these ideas and approaches can be incorporated in helping an individual reduce their distress and increase their QOL. What I have described in the previous chapters is also an easily understood method of assistance. If I see a client or a patient in practice, this is what I do. These procedures allow me to determine what kind of issues are confronting the person, how stressed they are, and some initial ideas about whether their stress response is proportional to the described stressors, or whether those five intervening variables are playing a large role. I have chosen a person with a particularly low QOL score to illustrate these points to the maximum. The same principles would take different forms with people having higher QOL scores. This method allows me to prioritize where assistance needs to begin and what steps to follow. Remember, though, that most people seen in practice are in various levels of distress and are not typical of the entire population. Nevertheless, nearly everyone has periods of high stress and negative experiences that these procedures can be applied to.

After introductions and the purpose of the visit has been explained, I quickly assess how stressed this person is, and what form it is taking - whether it is physical or psychological or both. Again, using Figure 15.1, I start with the right-hand and left-hand sides of the diagram. I want to know how stressed the person is and what the nature of the stressor is according to him or her. I am simultaneously evaluating his or her response while determining if the response is proportional to the stressor. If the person's stress response is so high that it meets the criteria for a psychiatric or psychological disorder, then we must first consider an evaluation for medication. At this time, I also gather information about such things as personal history, physical conditions, and medicines. And I will have them fill out their first QOL scale. If they agree, they are referred to a physician for an evaluation for medication. During the first appointment or the second, I begin to gather information about those five intervening factors we keep discussing. As is true in most cases, these five factors will be playing a very large role in this person's stress and negative experiences. You would be surprised how many people are not aware of the steps they have gone through to end up as stressed as they are.

I will never forget one woman who came to clinics because her arthritis had worsened and she was in more pain. She was seen by my partner, a family physician who noted that she was very stressed, but he didn't know why. When I saw her, I said, "Dr. B thinks you are very stressed right now. Is everything OK?" To which she said, "Yes." But of course, you have to dig a little deeper. So I said, "You haven't been in to see us for about a year. Tell me what changes have happened during the last year (change equals stressor)." To which she said, "My husband died last year, and because he died, I lost his pension. So I had to move away from my friends. And my son's fiancé called off their wedding, and he was so upset he tried to kill himself by jumping into the lion pit at the zoo. And my arthritis got worse." I thought the poor woman was so depressed that she could barely function. Obviously one of the first things we had to do was get her depression under better control with medication and tons of support. Clearly, she was looking to me to be a resource and provide support until she was better able to function. I fulfilled those needs for her. When we were able to get this woman's depression under better control, we could slowly move from a supportive role to a counseling role. For example, we would then examine the nature of her current stressors, and what she could do to reduce exposure to any of them. We then began to explore what sources of support she had available in her life, her feelings about her deceased husband, what she wanted in the future, what she was doing to cope with these tragic events, and what positive experiences she had in her life. When she was feeling stronger, I encouraged her, in my presence, to go through each of the four elements (physically, emotionally, behaviorally, and cognitively) of the way she was experiencing her grief and her sadness. This not only allowed her to express it, but also gave her an opportunity for the expression of other emotions or thoughts she might be having, such as anger, desertion, or fear. These, in turn, could be experienced and expressed and hopefully replaced with less negative and more positive experiences. Additionally, it was important to find some positive activities she could engage in while simultaneously reducing her stress and negative experiences. She started with a QOL of 1 out of 7 and six months later her QOL was 3 out of 7. This was a tremendous improvement in QOL which allowed her to eventually increase her QOL up to a 5 over the next year.

In this chapter, we have outlined a model of stress, described what it is, and the variables that affect it. We distinguished between stress as a response, and stressor as a stimulus or triggering event. We also noted that other than two relatively rare classes of stressors (which we labeled reflexive and selective), most stressors are of the interactive nature. That is, it is difficult to separate the stressor itself (such as traffic) from the five intervening variables that interact with it. Stress, like beauty, is usually in the eye of the beholder. We can reduce stress in several ways. When appropriate, we can take a medication to counteract the damage that stress produces in our body and our brain. Other methods, such as yoga, exercise, or improving nutrition will also directly reduce the stress response. We can avoid the triggering event or find a way to be exposed to it less frequently. Through various techniques we can learn to adjust some of our personality traits, change our view of potential stressors, change our coping methods, develop or improve social support systems, and learn to use whatever resources we have available. If we do all of these things correctly, our stress and resultant negative experiences can be reduced by at least 70%. Such a change would have a dramatic effect on QOL.

QOL AND CHALLENGING LIFE SITUATIONS

CHAPTER 19: QUALITY OF LIFE AND DISABILITY

In this chapter, I will discuss how quality of life is related to having a disability. I will draw upon some of the literature that I think is most relevant, draw upon our own model of quality of life, and share some of my own personal experiences regarding this topic. For those of you who are not familiar with the term "disability," I will take a few moments to explain it. According to the World Health Organization, a disability is a decrease in daily functioning that occurs because of a significant medical, sensory, or psychiatric impairment. An "impairment" means that there is a temporary or permanent disturbance in the normal functioning of an organ system. That organ system may be the brain, other parts of the nervous system, the musculoskeletal system, the cardiovascular system, the sensory systems, or any other major physical system of the body. For purposes of this chapter, I will include major psychiatric problems, such as schizophrenia, as being due to impairments in brain functioning. In most of the literature, these dysfunctions are labeled as impairments. A disability, on the other hand, is what results from these impairments. Disabilities or disruptions in functioning can occur in three different realms and can vary in the amount of dysfunction that occurs. These three realms are termed Activities of Daily Living (or ADLs), Instrumental Activities of Daily Living (IADLs), and thirdly, dysfunction at higher-order activities such as fulfilling social roles and employment. At any given time, approximately 13% of the US population is affected by a disability severe enough to interfere with functioning in at least one of these realms. The most common impairments causing disability include stroke, cardiovascular disease, respiratory diseases, impairments of the visual system and auditory system, arthritis, back injuries, spinal cord injuries, brain injuries, and birth defects. Populations of people very concerned about how these impairments affect quality of life include parents of children with a physical impairment such as cerebral palsy; adults with an injury, amputation, spinal cord injury, or sensory impairment; veterans returning from service with amputations, post-traumatic stress disorders, and blindness; and older adults with degenerative orthopedic or neurological conditions such as Parkinson's disease. Each of these populations and others sooner or later deals with the issue of how their impairment and resulting disability will impact their quality of life. In this chapter, I will try to show what factors are most responsible for having higher or lower QOL following a disability.

One of the most important points to remember is that quality of life among people with a disability appears to be due, at its core, to the same factors that are responsible for it in the nondisabled population. That is, quality of life will be determined by the relative balance of negative experiences to positive experiences. We do not need a separate theory of quality of life for people with a disability anymore than we need a separate theory of gravity for people with a disability. The basic issues are still the same. Another point we need to stress seriously is that people who have a disability have many more issues facing them that are likely to result in negative experiences than people without a disability. Third, obtaining and maintaining a sufficient number of positive experiences in the presence of a disability is usually more difficult because the person with the disability will face many more obstacles in the physical, environmental, and social aspects of life than a nondisabled person.

Disability and secondary conditions

The issue of primary disability and secondary conditions is very important in understanding quality of life issues. The term "secondary condition" refers to the many physical and psychological complications that come about as the result of a primary disability. While the recent literature debates the term "secondary condition" and offers various alternative definitions, I am simply going to call these collectively "secondary conditions." Perhaps the best way to explain these secondary conditions is to give several examples. People with blindness have many problems, obviously, due to the blindness, including the inability to find their way around, to read, or to see other people. The blindness is the primary impairment, while the inability to get around easily is a disability directly due to the blindness. However, several important secondary conditions also occur among this population. One of the most important is the high occurrence of fractures due to falling. The fractures are secondary conditions due to the primary impairment. They are not directly due to the blindness, but to the complications of the blindness. People who have a spinal cord injury have high rates of osteoporosis, which means a depletion of calcium in some of the major bones of the body. The osteoporosis is a secondary condition due to the spinal cord injury, while the paralysis could be termed the primary disability. Osteoporosis leads to many fractures in this group as well. Pain is an important secondary condition in most major physical impairments, including arthritis, back injuries, and amputation. Fatigue is also an important secondary condition that occurs frequently in many types of physical impairment, including polio, cerebral palsy, stroke, and spinal cord injury. Psychological depression is the most common secondary condition in all major impairment groups. It occurs in between 15 and 50% of people with a severe impairment at one time or another. Two important points need to be made about secondary conditions. The first is that many of these, if not all of them, can be prevented, minimized, or adequately treated. Second, secondary conditions are the cause of excess dysfunction at all levels of disability. When we talk about the impact of disability on quality of life, we need to remember that both the primary impairment and secondary conditions are equally important in contributing to quality of life. Finally, I have learned that psychological issues, ranging from depression to misconceptions about the value of oneself, are often the most important in contributing to quality of life.

Secondary conditions as the cause of negative experiences

We have pointed out that quality of life among people with a disability is the result of the relative balance between positive and negative experiences in life. Negative experiences are much more likely to occur in people who have a disability because of the great number of physical, psychological, and other complications and events which happen to them to contribute to negative experiences. Let us look at the wide range of these events which impinge upon the life of a person who has a disability. Remember from earlier chapters that we separate events from the experiences they may cause. Some events, such as pain, cause almost universal negative experiences. The same can be said for fatigue and medical complications. However, we must always be careful to understand how any event relates to negative experiences because people vary a great deal in how they interpret, cope with, and react to these events. The first category of secondary conditions likely to cause negative experiences is obviously those arising from physical causes. These include, as we mentioned, pain, fatigue, medical illnesses, and decreasing health over the long term. Each of these is far more likely among people with a disability than people without a disability.

The second category of secondary conditions is psychological. People with a disability have a high number and a great variety of psychological issues that they may face that impact their quality of life. These issues include acceptance of oneself as being different from either the way they were before or different from other people of similar age and background. A veteran returning from a war often is faced with accepting a different body image and self concept compared to before he or she was injured. People with a disability also have great concerns about how others will accept them, including the general public, family members, colleagues, and spouses. These feelings may result in being uncomfortable out in public with others, feeling as though they have to prove themselves to others at work, or concerns about keeping the love of a spouse or feeling guilty about needing care from others. The most severe form of psychological issue is the one we mentioned above – depression. The person with a disability may face changes in their health and functioning that occur at such a rapid rate that they are not able to aptly cope with them. The person who has a disability may also be faced with so many secondary conditions that they are difficult to cope with. For example, a person with a disability may need to cope with facing additional surgeries, having multiple periods of illness or just not feeling well, changes in sexual functioning, and changes in toileting that are more challenging than he or she is able to deal with. These multiple challenges and changes in one's physical condition and the occurrence of secondary physical problems predict the onset of depression. I know that I went through a period of depression following the onset of my progressive neurological illness because things were changing faster than I could cope with them. I was fortunate to recognize what was happening to me and got the proper assistance. When depression occurs, it will create its own set of negative experiences that the person may not be able to overcome without outside professional assistance.

Another major source of negative experiences facing a person with a disability are those that come from the physical environment. In this case we mean such things as difficulty crossing the street because of a lack of curb cuts or traffic lights that don't allow adequate time to cross, lack of adequate transportation for a person with a disability to be able to use, lack of proper access to public or private buildings, and lack of suitable office arrangements in doctors' offices to allow wheelchair access or ability to use an examining table. These physical aspects do not affect the life of a person without a disability nearly as much as they affect the life of people with a disability. These occurrences may result, and are even likely to result, in negative experiences for the disabled person that are experienced as frustration, anger, apathy, or lack of participation in the regular environment.

A fourth category of potential negative experiences facing a person with a disability, and a very potent one, is the social environment. Here I mean issues ranging from the general attitude of the public toward people who have a disability to specific interactions with individuals in the environment that result in feelings of devaluation or lack of respect on the part of the person with the disability. Let me give you a couple of examples. A friend of mine, a woman of middle age who uses a wheelchair, was accompanied by her husband to a department store to purchase a couple of new dresses. The store clerk, upon approaching the nondisabled husband and his wife, turned to the husband and asked him, "What size does she wear?" This unbelievable rudeness and lack of acceptance of the person in the wheelchair can be devastating. Unless the person with the disability has developed some good coping methods, such as telling the clerk, "I'm the one buying the dress, not him," or other suitable coping methods, this interaction can add to the number of negative experiences the person with the disability faces in a single day. In my own case, I have a private physician who I think is very caring and sensitive to most of my issues. However, in filling out prescription forms, he would often give them to my wife instead of to me, even in the days when I had adequate arm functioning. I pointed out to him that it was my prescription and would he please give it to me. He immediately recognized the inappropriateness of his actions and apologized. People who have a disability face innumerable challenges in the social environment such as these. Issues of lack of acceptance, devaluation, oversolicitation, or lack of thoughtfulness are likely to cause a high number of negative experiences.

Thus we can see that, between physical, functional,

environmental, and interpersonal events, the person with a disability is going to have a high number of negative experiences that will impact their quality of life. Not all people with a disability will be faced with all of these issues, but the majority of them will be. It is necessary to identify these negative experiences and their sources as an important step in improving quality of life.

What we know about QOL and disability

We know many important things about quality of life and disability based upon research conducted over the last 30 years. Much of this research, including some of my own, has been sponsored by the National Institute on Disability and Rehabilitation Research. I am personally glad to acknowledge their support of me over many years of research. I will discuss what we know, including the relationship of quality of life to primary impairment, secondary conditions, and disability, as each of these has important contributions to quality of life. Some of these findings may seem counterintuitive to begin with, and a little difficult to believe, but in fact are true.

Let's start by examining the relationship between quality of life and severity of primary impairment. Let us choose as our example results from the literature on spinal cord injury. Here, it is easy to see that there are different severities of primary impairment. A person may be paralyzed from the neck down, which we call tetraplegia, or maybe paralyzed from the waist down, which we call paraplegia. You might expect that people with paraplegia would have higher levels of quality of life than people with tetraplegia because of the different degrees of paralysis. However, the literature shows that measures of quality of life and life satisfaction are not very different between these two groups. This may seem to be a surprising result when you consider that people with tetraplegia are far more disabled than people with paraplegia and that they probably face many more challenges, but this result is due to the fact that it is not the primary impairment itself that is the cause of quality of life, as much as it is the secondary conditions, experiences, and other factors that we discussed above. This result holds true across other impairment groups, including polio, stroke, and arthritis. In order to fully understand why these results are possible, we will need to discuss how people with a physical disability are able to garner enough positive experiences to balance out all of the negative ones and thus have a satisfying life or even one of high quality. The results show that this is clearly possible because of how small the differences in quality of life are when based only upon severity of impairment. In my own case, I am paralyzed from the neck down and have only 5% vision in one eye. However, I rate my own quality of life at about 6. My physical impairments, while certainly a source of limitation and frequently frustration, have not kept me from finding enough positive experiences to overcome the negative experiences I have and to give me a fairly high quality of life.

The second thing we know about quality of life and disability is that neither the ability to perform Activities of Daily Living, nor the ability to perform Instrumental Activities of Daily Living, appear to be related to quality of life. You might expect that a person who could perform activities such as dressing, eating, grooming (ADLs), or driving, handling finances, or doing chores, would be more independent and therefore have a higher quality of life, but in fact this is also not true. Several studies, including many conducted by Krause,

Dijkers, Tate, and other people, have shown that the relationship between measures of quality of life and measures of basic independence is very low. The reason that these measures of basic independence are not related to measures of life satisfaction or quality of life to a higher extent is probably due to the fact that people do not derive very much satisfaction from being able to do these things because they can be assisted in many ways to accomplish them and because these do not provide much in the way of pleasure, success, or meaning if they can be accomplished. Remember, in our theory of quality of life, positive experiences include those in the categories of pleasure, success, and meaning. So a plausible explanation for the above findings is that not being able to accomplish these basic activities is not a major source of negative experiences, nor is being able to accomplish them a source of positive experience. They are simply things that need to be done and people find various ways to accomplish them.

On the other hand, the relationship between secondary conditions, or secondary disabilities, and quality of life is substantial. Of particular importance are the secondary conditions of depression, pain, fatigue, and secondary medical problems such as pneumonia, pressure sores, or fractures. Let me give you another example. The relationship between depression and level of spinal cord injury (tetraplegia vs. paraplegia) is very low. The frequency in each group is relatively the same. However, depression is strongly related to quality of life and may contribute as much as 50% to quality of life measures in individuals who are depressed. The reason for this is found in the way that depression contributes to having a high rate of negative experiences, and high rates of negative experiences contribute to low quality of life. Depression itself is a tremendously negative experience emotionally. People who have suffered with major depression will tell you that they never felt worse in their lives and that everything in their lives became negative. They could not sleep, get along with other people, find interest in any activities, or mobilize much energy to make it through the day. Moreover, being depressed would lead them to have more negative experiences and fewer positive experiences because they would not engage in any activities that would be a potential source of positive experience and they would frequently have arguments and upsets with others, which contributed more negative experiences. Again, depression is not caused by the primary impairment. Depression is never a normal response to having a severe impairment or severe disability. It is an abnormal, secondary condition, and one that not only should be treated, but can be treated. My colleagues and I demonstrated that depression among people with a severe physical impairment could be readily treated over a six month period and was improved significantly over just eight weeks. Likewise, we have found that pain, fatigue, and medical complications play a major role in contributing to low quality of life and lack of life satisfaction, even more than the primary impairment. Uncorrected physical pain, excess fatigue, and frequent medical setbacks are highly related to low quality of life, both because they are negative experiences in themselves and because, when they are present, they block access to many or most positive experiences. When a person has any of these secondary physical problems, it is difficult to imagine how they can feel like participating with others, enjoying everyday pleasures, or being able to work a full work shift. Thus we see that secondary conditions and secondary impairments are probably larger contributors to overall quality of life than is the primary impairment itself. Thankfully, most of the secondary conditions affecting people with disabilities can be eliminated or greatly minimized through proper treatment, prevention of conditions in the first place, the use of assistive devices and equipment, and careful planning of activities during the day to not exceed physical capacity.

Disability, quality of life, and positive experiences

We have so far discussed how primary impairment and basic activities of daily living are not strongly related to quality of life. We have also pointed out how secondary conditions, such as pain and depression, are strongly related to low quality of life because they are sources of negative experiences. Furthermore, we have discussed how the physical environment and the social environment may contribute to negative experiences for the person with a disability. Given all these factors, it might seem surprising that people who have a disability can have a positive quality of life at all. However, here again, research shows that, on average, there is only a small difference between people who have a disability and people who do not on measures of quality of life. That must mean that many people who have a disability have found ways of balancing these potential negative experiences with positive experiences. In this section we will again review the sources of positive experience in our theory, point out some of the difficulties people who have a disability initially face in achieving them, and how those who do obtain a high quality of life are able to include enough of these positive experiences.

In our model of quality of life, it should be noted that we

proposed three different kinds of positive experiences – pleasurable experiences, successful experiences, and meaningful experiences. We further proposed that a person with higher levels of quality of life has a higher number of these kinds of experiences compared to the number of negative experiences they have. Along these lines, Devins proposed in 1983 that higher quality of life would be related to restoring valued activities. We go further than that and say that these activities are valued because they provide one or more of these kinds of experiences. Devins did not state what activities would be valued by individuals because it is impossible to know without asking. We propose that whatever activities the person engages in after a disability must provide one or more of these kinds of experiences if they are going to contribute to a higher quality of life. We have found, like Devins, that when a disability occurs, people often have to make adjustments to what is important to them, as well as adjustments to the activities that are going to provide these experiences. Let me give you a further example of what I mean. Nondisabled people who are young or middle-aged derive much of their quality of life through activities that provide them pleasurable or successful experiences. They are often involved in employment, social groups, sporting activities, travel, or hobbies. When a disability occurs, especially a severe disability, people have a hard time adjusting to it because there are usually obstacles and barriers present that limit their ability to engage in the activities that provided them these positive experiences. Employment is frequently either difficult or unattainable, many sporting activities are no longer capable of being performed, travel may be difficult, and participation in social events may also be limited. How, then, are these people going to keep as high a level of quality of life as they had before? I have heard that many of the veterans returning from recent wars in the Middle East who have suffered a disability say that they find it very difficult to have as high a quality of life as they had before the war. We can see from what we already know about quality of life and disability that restoring the ability to perform Activities of Daily Living and even Instrumental Activities of Daily Living with these veterans is not sufficient to restore their quality of life. Frequently, new sources to achieve these positive experiences need to be found. We cannot assume as family members, friends, or professional therapists that proposing any particular activity will result in a positive experience for the person with a disability. It may take a great deal of work to identify new activities or new ways of performing old activities that will provide positive experiences. For example, a family member or spouse may suggest that it would be fun to go out to a movie as a source of enjoyment. They may be surprised by the lack of willingness on the part of the person with the disability to participate in that activity, but the person with the disability may look at that activity as a source of negative experience when it is difficult to find adequate parking, make it up a curb to get into the theater, or find accessible seating spaces in the theater complex. The potential negative experiences may outweigh whatever positive experiences can be gained by that activity. On the other hand, a positive experience may result either by exploring theaters that have adequate seating, by getting to the theater early to navigate other obstacles, or by renting a movie and enjoying it at home. What I mean by all of this is that there is no way to know at face value what activity will provide positive experiences for the individual with a disability. Instead, it may be more useful to ask the person who has a disability what provided them pleasure and success in the past and how might those experiences still be made available to them. This may occur by a total change in activities or a change in the way activities were done before. A person with a disability may have enjoyed a particular hobby that is nearly impossible to perform in the presence of the disability. However, there may be equipment or assistive devices available that would allow the person to continue with that hobby. In Devins' words, these hobbies may have been highly valued and continuation of them is important to contribute to a high quality of life.

Maintaining a sufficient number of successful experiences following a disability is one of the biggest challenges to quality of life because so often success is measured in terms of how much a person earns, what other things they achieve, their ownership of a home or a car, and whether others view them as successful or not. These are difficult challenges to be sure, especially when it is noted that only about 18% of people with a severe disability are employed, over 25% live in poverty, and fewer people with disabilities get married than those without disabilities. It is likely that people who have a disability also are less likely to own a home, own reliable transportation, or have access to the internet. These issues make it difficult to maintain a sense of success and to enjoy this as a source of quality of life for many people who have a disability. It is far easier to find new sources of pleasure and fun than it is to find new sources of success. As long as public policies and governmental actions and budgetary realities remain as they are, it is difficult to see how many of these conditions will objectively improve. However, that is not to say that a person who has a disability can't **experience** success by focusing on different definitions of success and different activities that can provide these experiences. For a child with a cognitive impairment, it is unlikely they will achieve at the same level in all subjects as their nondisabled counterparts. However, there is no reason why they cannot have a sense of success by focusing on tasks they can perform, by rewarding small advances in progress, and by comparing them to only their own level of performance and not to that of their nondisabled peers. It is also important that children who have a disability participate in social activities along with their nondisabled peers in order to have a measure of success by being accepted. Years ago, it was far more common for children who had a disability to go to separate schools away from their nondisabled peers. Among the wide range of negative effects of this practice was a sense of failure by not being accepted by others and a lack of feeling successful by interacting with nondisabled peers. Changes in this practice have allowed children with disabilities to feel more integrated and more successful in their daily lives. Feeling successful, for an adult with a disability, may not come about by being employed anymore, but may come about by managing activities at home which allow the spouse to go to work. This is frequently an exchange of roles that is difficult to accept at first, but if success is looked upon as benefiting the family unit, then it may be more positively accepted. Returning to school to advance one's education after a disability often leads to successful experiences when the individual cannot return to their previous work. Maintaining a successful social life with friends and with volunteer activities also contributes to successful experiences and to a higher quality of life.

The third source of positive experience, as you will remember, is meaningful or purposeful experiences. We have already described the nature of these in an earlier chapter. Here we want to point out the importance of these experiences in achieving a high quality of life for people who have a disability. There are two ways that meaningful experiences contribute to quality of life for a person with a disability. The first way is to see the meaning or value in everyday activities and how these contribute to an overall sense of improving one's recovery in the face of a new disability. The second way that meaningful activities contribute to a positive quality of life is during the long term phase of disability. Let me explain what I mean. During the initial phase of disability, when improvement and maximizing abilities is most important, finding meaning in ordinary activities such as being able to dress oneself, navigate the physical environment, or even to obtain a job are important if they contribute to the person's sense that he or she is improving. Here again, it is not the activity itself that is so important as it is the meaning the person attaches to being able to accomplish that activity or task. Let me give you another example. Wayne Gordon and his colleagues studied the effect of employment on quality of life among people with a relatively new brain injury. Among the variables they assessed were whether the person was employed or not, the percentage of time they were employed each week, their hourly wage, and the type of job. None of these objective variables were related to quality of life. However, quality of life was related to the meaningful interpretations these people attached to employment. People with the highest quality of life scores interpreted their employment as meaning that they were improving in their recovery, were being productive again, were returning to their old selves, or were being as good as ever. Thus, during the earliest stages of rehabilitation, being able to find meaning in activities, even employment, is related to having a higher quality of life.

Secondly, during the long term phase of disability, when a person is past recovering and improving as much as they are going to and when adjustment to the disability situation has stabilized, we have found that people who have the highest quality of life find meaning in the activities they do and engage in many activities only if they do cause a sense of meaning or purpose. Other authors have also noted a shift toward performing and engaging in activities because of their meaningfulness rather than for other reasons such as economic incentive or pleasure. This shift may be one toward increasing religiosity and finding more value and meaning in scripture than they had found before. It may manifest itself in volunteering as a mentor to other people. It may take the form of finding a job that is meaningful even if the pay is less than the person earned previously. Any way that it occurs, I believe that a greater proportion of quality of life among people with a disability comes from meaningful activities than it does for their age-matched nondisabled peers. Thus people who have a long term disability and who have the highest levels of quality of life have a combination of positive experiences that include a healthy number of meaningful activities as well as the presence of pleasurable experiences and successful experiences.

Now, what does all this mean if you are a person with a new disability or one that you've had for a number of years? First, if you are a person with a new disability, I would concentrate on ways to deal with all of the negative experiences you are bound to have while trying to also have as many pleasurable and successful experiences as you can during this initial period. You may find yourself overwhelmed with negative experiences to the extent that you need assistance coping with them. This would be especially true if you find that you have become depressed. You can help to determine whether or not you have become depressed by taking the depression questionnaire in Appendix G. During this phase, you may find that very few things give you pleasure or a sense of success. However, keep trying to identify activities or events that can provide you with pleasure, as this is the easiest form of positive experience to have and this will help to balance out some of the negative experiences you are having. Also, be sure to set reasonable goals for yourself in terms of improving various functions such as getting dressed, walking, or navigating your wheelchair (if you use one). Setting small goals will help you to have a sense of success when you achieve them. Also try to find meaning or purpose in the disability experience. Perhaps there are some positives about having a disability that you did not recognize previously. Maybe it brings a better understanding of others who are going through very difficult times themselves, whether it is caused by a disability, or an earthquake, or the loss of loved ones. You may find yourself being more able to empathize with the difficulties of others. As you improve in your functioning and recovery, begin to improve your quality of life by including all three kinds of positive experiences in your life on a weekly basis. For people who have a long term disability, if your quality of life is not what you would like it to be, then the previous chapters in this book are relevant for you. There is no need to think a different approach to improving quality of life than the one presented here is necessary. Whatever your circumstances, your ultimate quality of life will still be determined by the balance of negative and positive experiences you bring into your life.

CONCLUDING COMMENTS AND RESOURCES

CHAPTER 20: SUMMARY, CONCLUSIONS, AND CONJECTURES

In summary

The purpose of this book was to help improve the quality of life of individuals regardless of their current circumstances. Whether you are an average individual wishing to improve your quality of life, a person wondering if life is giving you all that it should, or if you are a person with difficult circumstances, this book was designed to help you improve your quality of life. This book drew a distinction between subjective quality of life and the objective circumstances of one's life. The objective circumstances of one's life can be measured by noting the presence or absence of certain indicators such as type of employment, amount of income, level of education, health status, home ownership, marital status, and other variables. These objective indicators are currently said to measure one's standard of living. One's quality of life, however, is measured by their experiences in and of life. Research shows that there is a surprisingly low relationship between one's standard of living and one's quality of life. A person may have a very high standard of living, but could still have a relatively low quality of life. On the other hand, a person could have a relatively low standard of living and have a pretty high quality of life. Interestingly, the standard of living of individuals in the United States has improved dramatically from the year 1900 until the present time, while there has been relatively little change in people's quality of life since about 1960. More people have gained ownership of a home, possession of a car, higher income, better health, and more education since the turn of the last century. However, there has not been as much increase in people's sense of the quality of their lives. This book was designed to help restore higher levels of quality of life that many people appear to be searching for.

The basic tenet of the theory of quality of life used in this book is that quality of life depends upon the relative balance of positive and negative experiences one has in life. This model of quality of life focused on three kinds of negative experiences and three kinds of positive experiences that are believed to be important to all individuals across different ages, levels of income, and across cultures. Experiences that are distressing, of a physical, psychological, or interpersonal nature, have a negative impact on everyone. On the other hand, the presence of pleasurable, successful, or meaningful experiences are positive for everyone. The idea of an experience in this book means how someone reacts with their feelings, thoughts, and actions to a particular event, situation, or activity. While the three distressing forms of negative experiences are nearly universal, people vary a lot in terms of the kinds of activities or events that bring them a sense of pleasure, success, or meaning. This book shows how to gain more positive experiences and therefore increase one's quality of life. This book contains questionnaires to help gauge one's current levels of negative and positive experiences. It then describes methods for reducing negative experiences in life and methods for improving positive experiences. Evidence shows that people are able to assess where they stand in regard to each of these kinds of experiences. This book also proposes that the same theory of quality of life can be applied to individuals with even more severe circumstances, such as people who have a disability, who live in relative poverty, or who face difficult family or social problems. Improving one's quality of life can occur over a relatively short period of time with proper guidance. By following the recommendations in this book, one can expect to improve their quality of life in anywhere between four and eight months, depending upon their current situation and how closely they follow the steps recommended in the book.

Conclusions

People are not inherently trapped in their current sense of their quality of life, despite the circumstances in which they live. Much can be done to improve one's quality of life and to see how it is not a direct result of their surrounding circumstances. From our reactions to driving in bumper-to-bumper traffic, to our overall sense of how our lives are going, we are capable of making substantial changes to the events in our lives that will give us a greater sense of control and a higher quality of life. Finding ways to improve the number of pleasurable, successful, and meaningful experiences in our lives is the surest route to having a higher quality of life. Sure, it would be wonderful to have as much money as we desire in order to provide ourselves with better homes, better cars, and exciting trips. But those things alone do not guarantee a high quality of life. Instead, by focusing on the kinds of experiences of a positive nature that anyone can learn about and promote, each of us can improve our own quality of life. People with the highest quality of life have learned how to minimize the negative experiences in their lives while maintaining a high, balanced level of positive experiences. When one is able to separate their **objective** situation from their **experiences** of their situation, then they can gain the freedom to control and improve their lives. This means learning that how we feel, what we think, and how we act are not due to the situations in our lives, such as an encounter with another person or being terminated from a job. Nothing makes us respond in any particular way to these situations. We can learn to interpret these situations and others in a way that will give us more control over our own reactions, a wider range of ways we can experience these situations, and a higher quality of life, or at least a less negative quality of life. By the same token, we can learn to create the positive experiences in our lives that will allow us all to have a more positive and higher quality of life for ourselves and others.

Conjectures

A national quality of life survey. Each year, the government spends millions of dollars conducting research, or having it conducted by universities, to assess the Gross National Product, employment statistics, and a variety of other measures designed to determine the objective well-being of the country and of the people living in it. I propose that, in addition to these very helpful objective measures, there also be an equivalent assessment of the subjective quality of life that people experience. This assessment would do much to tell us about how people rate their lives, how it may change from year to year, and how it may or may not relate to all of the objective measures that are gathered. I have a feeling that the government makes the same mistake that many individuals make – it believes that improvements in objective circumstances in people's lives and in the country as a whole will automatically lead to an increase in the quality of life of individuals. This is the same mistake many people make when they falsely believe that their sense of their overall quality of life is determined by the objective events and conditions in their lives. A national survey would allow us to determine how many people rate their quality of life as low and therefore must have a preponderance of negative experiences in their lives, and how many people rate their quality of life as high and therefore must be having a preponderance of positive experiences. Maybe then funding could be directed toward alleviating these negative experiences in lives, such as by improving mental health services or by funding more educational programs that promote how to improve positive experiences in life.

Having a positive quality of life takes time. Here, I do not mean that it takes a long time to increase one's quality of life, but instead, it takes time to fully experience the elements that contribute to a positive quality of life. You cannot go through life at a fast pace and hope to experience very much when you consider that the definition of experiencing anything means to be able to recognize the feelings that are present, the thoughts that occur to you, the way that your body feels, and the way that you act in relation to pleasant, successful, or meaningful experiences. A person who rushes through life, going from one activity to the next activity and from one event to the next event, cannot participate in all of these elements because it takes time to do so. You cannot quickly listen to Mozart's violin concertos in rapid succession and hope to gain all that you can from this activity. Instead, it is necessary to focus on the feelings resulting from the music, the way it makes you react in your body, the thoughts that occur to you, and your actions at the time. Finding the meaning, or value, and the pleasure in doing a kind deed for someone else takes time. A person who is too time-conscious and feels as though they must work harder and faster to keep up with life will have a hard time getting what they could get from such encounters.

Quality of life is the same across cultures. I don't know of any research on this topic, but I am inclined to believe, based upon my studies of anthropology, that all cultures define positive experiences in the same way. That is, in all cultures, there are events or activities that lead to the experiences of pleasure, success, or meaning. Individuals in all societies have found activities, events, and rituals that provide these three basic kinds of positive experience. Whether it is the pleasure brought about by a particular favorite meal, the success experienced by bringing back game for the tribe, or the meaningfulness of participation in rite of passage ceremonies, all cultures appear to me to have the same things which contribute to their quality of life. Research along these lines would be very helpful and would demonstrate how each of us is looking for the same things in life that will increase our quality of life.

People who derive most of their positive experiences through meaning, purpose, and value have the highest quality of life. I do not have enough data to confirm this idea, but it seems to me from what I have observed of people that individuals who have a strong philosophical, religious, or spiritualistic leaning in life have the highest levels of quality of life. The reason I believe this is that people with these orientations have a broad philosophical view of life and their place in it that allows them to interpret all of the events that occur to them within this philosophical system. A person with a strong religious background will see how life around them and the events which occur have meaning and purpose to them. Therefore even supposedly negative events can be seen as occurring for a greater reason and this may minimize their impact. I have seen people suffer with the pain of cancer courageously and minimize its impact by believing that they were in the final stages of embarking toward heaven. I have also seen how elderly individuals take great pride in being able to interact with their grandchildren, especially if they have a strong philosophical view of the natural course of life and its ongoing stages. On the other hand, I have seen many older individuals who thought that their grandchildren were an annoyance because they had no such view of the continuity of life, but were only focused on the present time and whether the grandchildren were requiring too much time, attention, or expenditures. Experiences of meaning and purpose can be instrumental in leading to a higher quality of life.

ACKNOWLEDGEMENTS

The author is pleased to thank and acknowledge many people who helped to make this book possible. First, I would like to thank my close friends and colleagues, Jason Kahan, Leonard Matheson, Michael Plopper and Rodney Adkins. Their reviews of each chapter and their assistance in clarifying the material is much appreciated. Their help in conducting research studies for purposes of this book helped greatly. I would like to also acknowledge the work of my research assistants, Julie Lutz, Keiko Kono, and Adam Bateham, for their untiring help in manuscript preparation, checking of references, and editing. I would also like to acknowledge the National Institute on Disability and Rehabilitation Research who funded my research program for more than 25 years. Their support provided the financial resources needed for studying changes occurring to people with disability as they age. It was by studying lifelong adaptations that the importance of developing a high quality of life became evident. Finally, I would like to acknowledge the loving support my wife, Cheryl, provided to me during the long and sometimes arduous tasks involved in preparing this book.

RESOURCES

This chapter is divided into two parts. One part gives a list of additional resources you may turn to, if you choose, for expanded explanations and examples of the material in specific chapters. This allows you to pick and choose among a variety of topics you may find interesting. The second part of this chapter is a list of references that were used in the preparation of this book. Many of these are scientific articles that provide some of the supporting evidence for the content of this book. These references were not cited throughout the book, in order to keep the book less "scientific looking" and more "user friendly."

Recommended Books and Resources

The Goaling Kit by Leonard Matheson, PhD.

One of Dr. Kemp's longtime colleagues uses the Quality of Life Rating Scale in a fun activity to help you identify your life goals. Goaling uses goals that reflect your values in a Life Plan that can be shared with others. The Goaling Kit contains the essential materials needed to complete the Goaling process and develop a values-based Life Plan. Sharing your goals with others helps improve motivation and accountability. Information and materials to implement Goaling can be found at www.GoalingInstitute.com.

Frankl, V. E. (1963). Man's search for meaning: An introduction to logotherapy. Boston: Beacon Press.

This is a must-read book for anyone interested in how one successfully deals with the most despairing conditions in life. Frankl describes survival in a Nazi concentration camp and making sense of it in the lives of survivors by putting it in a context of meaning and personal power.

Jung, C. G., Read, H. E., Fordham, M. S. M., & Adler, G. (1953). *The collected works of C.G. Jung.* Bollingen series, 20. New York: Pantheon Books.

This set of classic papers describes Carl Jung's insightful glimpse into the connection between personality and spiritual forces operating universally. The spiritual forces are described as archetypes and they shape and mold our personalities in accord to their principles. Jung thought that the symbolism of artwork, dreams, dance, and other actions were representatives of these archetypes.

McClelland, D. C. (1961). *The achieving society.* Princeton, N.J.: Van Nostrand.

This classic book describes man's need to achieve. The authors describe measurement and meaning of achievement motivation and how it displays itself at work and at home. It is important in our context because achievement and accomplishment are important positive experiences related to QOL.

Vash, C. L., & Crewe, N. M. (2004). *Psychology of disability.*

Springer series in rehabilitation. New York: Springer Pub.

This book is by well known authors who takes the reader through various stages of life from a disability perspective. This book contains both good common sense and thought provoking ideas. This book should be a requirement for all professionals working with people who have a disability as well as people with a disability themselves.

Other Recommended Books

Allen, J. (1977). *As a man thinketh*. Alhambra, Calif.: Miller Books.

Batchelor, S. (2008). *Buddhism without Beliefs: a Contemporary Guide to Awakening*. London: Bloomsbury.

Bronowski, J. (1974). *The ascent of man*. Boston: Little, Brown.

Campbell, J. (1988). *The Power of Myth*. New York, N.Y.: Random House.

Coelho, P., & Clarke, A. (2002; 1993). *The alchemist* [Alquimista.]. San Francisco: HarperSanFrancisco.

Easterbrook, G. (2003). *The progress paradox: How life gets better while people feel worse*. New York: Random House.

Ende, M., & Brownjohn, M. (1985). *Momo*. London: Puffin.

Fulghum, R. (1988). *All I really need to know I learned in kindergarten : Uncommon thoughts on common things* (1st ed.). New York: Villard Books.

Gaarder, J. (1994). *Sophie's world : A novel about the history of philosophy* [Sofies verden.] (1st ed.). New York: Farrar, Straus and Giroux.

Goldberg, B. (Ed.) (1988).*The Talmud*. Jerusalem, Israel: The Israel Institute for Talmudic Publications.

Goldratt, E. M., & Cox, J. (1992). *The goal : A process of ongoing improvement* (2 rev ed.). Croton-on-Hudson, NY: North River Press.

Gunaratana, H. (2002). *Mindfulness in Plain English*. Boston: Wisdom Publications.

Hawking, S. W. (1988). *A brief history of time : From the big bang to black holes*. Toronto ; New York: Bantam Books.

Kabat-Zinn, J. (2005). *Wherever You Go, There You Are: Mindfulness Meditation in Everyday Life*. New York: Hyperion.

Kamo, C., Moriguchi, Y., & Jenkins, D. (1996). *Hojoki, Visions of a Torn World*. Berkeley, CA: Stone Bridge.

Kapleau, P. (2000). *The Three Pillars of Zen: Teaching, Practice, and Enlightenment*. New York: Anchor.

Laozi. (1994). *Tao Te Ching*. New York: Knopf.

Laozi, & Wei, H. (1982). *The Guiding Light of Lao Tzu: a New Translation and Commentary on the Tao Teh Ching*. Wheaton, IL: Theosophical Pub. House.

Liezi, & Wong, E. (2001). *Lieh-tzu: a Taoist Guide to Practical Living*. Boston: Shambhala.

Miyamoto, M. (1982). *A Book of Five Rings*. Woodstock, N.Y.: Overlook.

Pausch, R., & Zaslow, J. (2008). *The Last Lecture*. New York: Hyperion.

Peters, T. J. (1999). *The Project50, Or, Fifty Ways to Transform Every Task into a Project That Matters!* New York: A.A. Knopf.

Pirsig, R. M. (1974). *Zen and the art of motorcycle maintenance: An inquiry into values*. New York: Morrow.

Sagan, C. (1975). *Cosmos*. New York: Ballantine.

Saint-Exupéry, A. D., & Howard, R. (2000). *The Little Prince*. San Diego: Harcourt.

Seligman, M. (2002). *Authentic Happiness*. New York, N.Y.: The Free Press.

Warren, R. (2002). *The purpose driven life*. Michigan: Zondervan.

Whitman, W., & Murphy, F. (2004). *The Complete Poems*. London: Penguin.

REFERENCES

Andrews, F. (1983). Population issues and social indicators of well-being. *Population & Environment: Behavioral & Social Issues, 6*(4), 210-230.

Andrews, F. (1991). Stability and change in levels and structure of subjective well-being: USA 1972 and 1988. *Social Indicators Research, 25*(1), 1-30.

Barker, R.N., Kendall, M.D., Amsters, D.I., Pershouse, K.J., Haines, T.P., & Kuipers, P. (2009). The relationship between quality of life and disability across the lifespan for people with spinal cord injury. *Spi nal Cord, 47, 149-155.*

Birren, J. E. (1964). *The psychology of aging.* Englewood Cliffs, N.J.: Prentice-Hall.

Bishop, M. (2005). Quality of life and psychosocial adaptation to chronic illness and acquired disability: a conceptual and theoretical synthesis. *The Journal of Rehabilitation, 1-17.*

Brown, A., 1996, The Social Processes of Aging and Old Age (2nd Ed.). Prentice Hall, New Jersey.

Camfield, L., & Skevington, S. M., (2008). On Subjective Well-being and Quality of Life. *Journal of Health Psychology, 13(6), 764-775.*

Campbell, A., Converse, P. E., & Rodgers, W. L. (1976). The quality of American life: Perceptions, evaluations, and satisfactions.

New York: Russell Sage Foundation.

Campbell, J., & Moyers, B. D. (1988). *The power of myth*. New York: Doubleday.

Campbell, M.L., Sheets, D., & Strong, P.S. (1999). Secondary health conditions among middle-aged individuals with chronic physical disabilities: Implications for unmet needs for services. *Assistive Technology, 11*(2), 105-122.

Center for Research on Women with Disabilities (CROWD). (2009). Psychosocial Health – Intimate Relationships. Retrieved from http://www.bcm.edu/crowd/?pmid=1423

Crewe, N.M. (1980). Quality of life: the ultimate goal in rehabilitation. *Minn Med, 586-589.*

deRoon-Cassini, T.A., de St. Aubin, E., Valvano, A., Hastings, J., & Horn, P. (2009). Psychological Well-Being After Spinal Cord Injury: Perception of Loss and Meaning Making. *Rehabilitation Psychology, 54(3), 306-314.*

Devins, G., et al. (1983). The emotional impact of end-stage renal disease: Importance of patients' perceptions of intrusiveness and control. *International Journal of Psychiatry in Medicine, 13*(4), 327-343.

Dijkers, M. (1997). Quality of life after spinal cord injury: A meta-analysis of the effects of disablement components. *Spinal Cord, 35(12) 829-840.*

Dijkers, M. (1999). Measuring Quality of Life: Methodological Issues. *American Journal of Physical Medicine & Rehabilitation, 78, 286-300.*

Duggan, C., & Dijkers, M. (2001). Quality of life after spinal cord injury: A qualitative study. *Rehabilitation Psychology, 46*(1),

REFERENCES

3-27.

Erikson, E., 1980. Identity and the Life Cycle. New York. Norton.

Flanagan, J. (1978). A research approach to improving our quality of life. *American Psychologist, 33*(2), 138-147.

Flanagan, J.C., 1979, Identifying opportunities for improving the quality of life of older age groups. California: American Institutes for Research.

Frankl, V. E. (1963). *Man's search for meaning; An introduction to logotherapy.* Boston: Beacon Press.

Freud, S., Freud, S., & Strachey, J. (1966). *The complete introductory lectures on psychoanalysis* [Vorlesungen zur Einführung in die Psychoanalyse.]. New York: W. W. Norton.

Fuhrer, M.J. (1992). Relationship of life satisfaction to impairment, disability and handicap among persons with spinal cord injury living in the community. *Archives of Physical Medicine and Rehabilitation, 73, 552-557.*

Fuhrer, M.J. (1996). The subjective well-being of people with spinal cord injury: relationships to impairment, disability and handicap. *Top Spinal Cord Injury Rehabilitation, 1, 56-71.*

Hammell, K. W. (2007). Quality of life after spinal cord injury: a meta-synthesis of qualitative findings. *Spinal Cord, 45, 124-139.*

Harari, Y.N. (2008). Combat Flow: Military, Political, and Ethical Dimensions of Subjective Well-Being in War. *Review of General Psychology, 12(3), 253-264.*

Heasley, S. (2011, September 14). More than 1 in 4 with disabilities living in poverty. *Disability Scoop.* Retrieved from http://www.disabilityscoop.com/2011/09/14/more-1-in-4-

poverty/13952/

Herzberg, F. (1968). One more time: how do you motivate employees?. *Harvard Business Review*, *46* (1), 53–62.

Herzberg, F., Mausner, B. & Snyderman, B.B. (1959). *The Motivation to Work.* New York: John Wiley.

Kahan, J., Mitchell, J., Kemp, B., & Adkins, R. (2006). The results of a 6-month treatment for depression on symptoms, life satisfaction, and community activities among individuals aging with a disability. *Rehabilitation Psychology*, *51*(1), 13-22.

Katz, P.P. &Yelin, E.H. (2001). Activity Loss and the Onset of Depressive Symptoms: Do Some Activities Matter More Than Others. *Arthritis & Rheumatism, 44(5), 1194-1202.*

Kemp, B. J., & Krause, J. S. (1999). Depression and life satisfaction among people aging with post-polio and spinal cord injury. *Disability & Rehabilitation, 21*, 241-249.

Kemp, B., & Mosqueda, L. A. (2004). <u>Aging with a disability: What the clinician needs to know</u>. Baltimore: Johns Hopkins University Press.

Krause, J.S., Kemp, B., Coker, J. (2000). Depression after spinal cord injury: Relation to gender, ethnicity, aging, and socioeconomic indicators. *Archives of Physical Medicine & Rehabilitation, 81, 1099-1109.*

MacPhillamy, D., & Lewinsohn, P. (1982). The pleasant events schedule: Studies on reliability, validity, and scale intercorrelation. *Journal of Consulting and Clinical Psychology*, *50*(3), 363-380.

McClelland, D. C. (1961). *The achieving society*. Princeton, N.J.: Van

REFERENCES

Nostrand.Middleton, J., Tran, Y., & Craig, A. (2007). Relationship Between Quality of Life and Self-Efficacy in Persons with Spinal Cord Injuries. *Arch Phys Med Rehabil, 88, 1643-1648.*

Poulin, M., & Silver, R. C. (2008). World Benevolence Beliefs and Well-Being Across the Life Span. *Psychology and Aging, 23(1), 13-23.*

Rapley, M. (2003). Quality of Life Research. California: Sage Publications.

Saunders, W.B. (2002). Quality of Life Measurement: Applications in Health & Rehabilitation Populations. *Archives of Physical Medicine and Rehabilitation, 83(12), 1-54.*

Schaie, K., & Parham, I. (1976). Stability of adult personalit traits: Fact or fable? *Journal of Personality and Social Psychology, 34*(1), 146-158.

Sheey, G., 1976. *Passages: Predictable Crises of Adult Life.* Dutton, New York.

Thompson, K. (2002). *Depression and Disability: A Practical Guide.* Chapel Hill, NC: NC Office on Disability and Health.

Tsaousides, T., Warshowsky, A., Ashman, T.A., Cantor, J.B., Spielman, L., & Gordon, W.A. (2009). The Relationship Between Employment-Related Self-Efficacy and Quality of Life Following Traumatic Brain Injury. *Rehabilitation Psychology, 54(3), 299-305.*

U.S. Department of Health and Human Services, Centers for Disease Control and Prevention, National Center for Health Statistics. (2012). *Summary health statistics for U.S. adults: National Health Interview Survey, 2010* (Vital and Health Statistics,

Series 10, Number 252).

U.S. Department of Labor, Bureau of Labor Statistics. (2012). *Persons with a disability: Labor force characteristics 2011* (News release June 8).

Vash, C. L., & Crewe, N. M. (2004). *Psychology of disability*. Springer series in rehabilitation. New York: Springer Pub.

APPENDIX A: POSITIVE EXPERIENCES INVENTORY

This inventory was designed to help you assess how many positive experiences you have during a typical week, and the nature of those experiences. There are no right or wrong answer to the questionnaire. After you completed, we will describe what your scores mean in regard to your QOL. We want you to think back over the last seven days and clearly picture those days and nights in your mind until you are 90% certain you can remember them. Then, simply answer the following three questions:

1) During the last week, how many times did you have the experience of pleasure or things related to that experience such as fun, enjoyment, excitement, or physical enjoyment, regardless of what activities you were doing at the time?

Place number here_____

2) How many times, during the last week, did you have the experience of accomplishing something or experiences similar to that such as a sense of achievement, success, recognition, productivity, or competence?

Place number here_____

3) How many times, during the last week, did you experience your life as meaningful, purposeful, important, or of value?

Place the number here _____

Please add together your scores.

Total Score_____

Which kind of experience is the <u>most important</u> for you?

Please circle the one that is most important for you:

1 (Pleasurable)   2 (Successful)   3 (Meaningful)

©1/13/12

APPENDIX B: NEGATIVE EXPERIENCES INVENTORY

This inventory was designed to help you assess how many negative experiences you have during a typical week, and the nature of those experiences. There is no right or wrong answer to the inventory. After you complete it, we will describe what your scores mean in regard to your QOL. We want you to think back over the last seven days and clearly picture those days and nights in your mind until you are 90% certain you can remember them. If this past week was highly unusual in that there were major traumas, such as death of family, onset of illness, or some other major events, please take this inventory three weeks from now. Please answer the following three questions.

1) During the last week, how many times did you have experiences of physical distress including (but not limited to) pain, fatigue, digestive problems, weakness, or difficulty with daily physical tasks?

      Place number here_____

2) How many times in the last week did you experience psychological distress such as depression, anxiety, panic, worry, sadness, guilt, or confusion?

      Place number here_____

3) How many times during the last week did you have the experience of conflict with others, isolation, lacking support, exclusion, alienation, or rejection?

Place the number here_____

Please add together your scores.

Total Score_____

APPENDIX C: PLEASURABLE EVENT SCHEDULE

1. Planning trips or vacations
2. Being at the beach
3. Watching movies at home
4. Going to a sports event
5. Watching TV
6. Camping
7. Laughing
8. Going to a party
9. Taking a nap
10. Watching wild animals
11. Wearing new clothes
12. Going to a fair, carnival, circus, zoo, or amusement park
13. Getting massages or backrubs
14. Watching the sky, clouds, stars, moon, or a storm
15. Going on outings (to the park, a picnic, or a barbecue, etc.)
16. Wearing clean clothes
17. Hearing jokes
18. Going to a health club, sauna bath, spa, etc.
19. Thinking about people I like
20. Having daydreams
21. Going to the movies
22. Being at a family reunion or get-together

23. Going to a restaurant
24. Seeing or smelling a flower or plant
25. Being invited out
26. Visiting friends
27. Giving massages or backrubs
28. Being relaxed
29. Playing board games (Monopoly, Scrabble, etc.)
30. Listening to music
31. Petting, necking, kissing
32. Amusing people
33. Reading books or magazines
34. Going to the library
35. Bird-watching
36. Watching people
37. Being with happy people
38. Talking about my hobby or special interest
39. Watching attractive women or men
40. Smiling at people
41. Being with my husband or wife
42. Going on field trips
43. Having coffee, tea, a coke, etc., with friends.
44. Doing things with children
45. Eating snacks
46. Reading cartoons, comic strips, or comic books
47. Seeing old friends
48. Traveling
49. Attending a concert, opera, or ballet
50. Playing with pets

APPENDIX D: SUCCESSFUL EVENT SCHEDULE

1. Taking tests when well prepared
2. Being able to work at home via computers
3. Completing a difficult task
4. Solving a personal problem
5. Making a major purchase or investment (car, appliance, house, stocks, etc.)
6. Getting a job advancement (being promoted, given a raise,-or offered a better job, accepted into a better school, etc.)
7. Working with others as a team
8. Being complimented or told I have done well
9. Winning a competition
10. Saying something clearly
11. Using my cell-phone to improve work
12. Speaking a foreign language
13. Going to a business meeting or convention
14. Writing papers, essays, articles, reports, memos, etc.
15. Doing a job well
16. Pleasing employers, teachers, etc.
17. Learning to do something new
18. Budgeting my time
19. Being praised by people I admire
20. Being asked for my help or advice

21. Winning an argument

22. Finishing a project or task

23. Learning a new computer program

24. Using my strength

25. Driving skillfully

26. Planning or organizing something

27. Repairing things

28. Teaching someone

29. Taking on-line classes

30. Reading a "How to Do It" book or article

31. Working on machines, (cars, bikes, motorcycles, tractors, etc.)

32. Writing stories, novels, plays or poetry

33. Working on my job

34. Reading essays or technical, academic, or professional literature

35. Giving a speech or lecture

36. Reading maps

37. Improving my health (having my teeth fixed, getting new glasses, changing my diet, etc.)

38. Doing "odd jobs" around the house

39. Coaching someone

40. Receiving honors (civic, military, etc.)

41. Doing experiments or other scientific work

42. Starting a new project

43. Telling people what to do

44. Having people show interest in what I have said

45. Solving a problem, puzzle, crossword, etc.

46. Having an original idea

47. Playing in a sporting competition

48. Winning a bet

49. Receiving money

50. Resolving a long standing interpersonal problem

APPENDIX E: MEANINGFUL EVENT SCHEDULE

1. Reading the Scriptures or other sacred works
2. Talking about philosophy or religion
3. Writing a personal journal or diary
4. Helping someone
5. Creating a family tree
6. Feeling the presence of the Lord in my life
7. Being told I am needed
8. Saying prayers
9. Writing to the congress about the issue important to you
10. Confessing or apologizing
11. Suffering for a good cause
12. Protesting social, political, or environmental conditions
13. Buying an American Flag for a display on holidays
14. Planting a tree in a honor of someone
15. Remembering a departed friend or loved one, visiting the cemetery
16. Being told I am loved
17. Having family members or friends do something that makes me proud of them
18. Doing volunteer work; working on community service projects
19. Having a meaningful conversation with someone
20. Going to service, civic, or social club meetings

21. Thinking about other people's problems

22. Making contributions to religious, charitable, or other groups

23. Being at weddings, baptisms, confirmations, etc.

24. Talking to a sick friends

25. Visiting people who are sick, shut in, or in trouble

26. Going to spiritual places

27. Seeing good things happen to my family or friends

28. Writing my autobiography

29. Donating my time to a worthy cause

30. Sending a card to a sick friend

31. Hearing a good sermon

32. Reading an inspirational book

33. Helping someone to complete the project

34. Mentoring a child in elementary school

35. Setting a good example for my family

36. Counseling someone with a problem

37. Meditating

38. Visiting memorable places

39. Giving blood to Red Cross

40. Restoring a family heirloom

APPENDIX F: GOAL ATTAINMENT SCHEDULE – WHAT WOULD IT TAKE?

Directions:

This schedule is designed to help you attain things you said would improve your QOL one unit. This goal attainment approach is an addition to what is mentioned in the next chapter and this method is more self-directed than the techniques in the next chapter. We will guide you through several steps in the current method but leave most of the work up to you. Check the box every time you complete each step.

1. Write down what you said to yourself about what it would take to move you one step higher on the QOL scale. Write it on the line below.

_____

☐   Date_____

2. Sharpen the statement by eliminating ambiguous terms. For example, if you said you want to "feel better" what does that mean? Be as precise as you can. Does it mean you want to have less pain, have a better mood, or be able to walk further? As much as possible,

put your statement in objective terms and rewrite it here.

☐   Date_____

3. Sharpen your statement again by making the end result something you want it to be that is under your control. For example, if you said you want a job, getting a job is not totally under your control. Sometimes there are no jobs available. However, if you restate your goal as "to position myself to be a highly desirable candidate for a job," that is under your control. You can get the training, consultation, networking, wardrobe, and resume redo that you need to be ready for a job.

☐   Date _____

4. Set the date that you have to have your goal accomplished. It should be no more than 6 months. Otherwise, you have chosen a goal that is more than one unit increase. Put the date here.

☐   Date_____

Now, put the date and your goal on ten 2x2 sticky notes and put them various places around the house where you will see them. These will strengthen your intentions and motivations to accomplish your goal.

5. Look at the score you got on the original QOL scale (not on the converted one). If you got a 1 or 2, I am sorry, but you cannot go further with this exercise. You must go to the next chapter and read the instructions pertaining to the score you received. If you scored 3 or higher, please proceed.

☐   Date_____

6. Most substantial tasks in life, such as the one you are attempting, usually require something from others, whether it is information, advice, basic emotional support, or monetary assistance. List here who and what could help you to formulate and carry out your action steps (next item).

_____

☐   Date_____

7. Break your goal down into between 5 to 7 mini steps. Every goal is made up of several steps which must be carried out in sequence. List these steps in proper sequence below. The last step should be the attainment of the goal.

☐   1) _____   Date_____

GOAL ATTAINMENT SCHEDULE

☐   2) _____   Date_____

☐   3) _____   Date_____

☐   4) _____   Date_____

☐   5) _____   Date_____

☐   6) _____   Date_____

☐   7) _____   Date_____

8. As you complete each mini step, put the date next to it.
Check the box when you complete each mini step.

9. Have you attained your goal? Yes or No?

If yes, congratulations! You have now improved your QOL and now you can continue to do so.

If no, look over the process above and figure out which step went wrong. Redo that step and continue toward your goal.

APPENDIX G: THE KEMP DEPRESSION ASSESSMENT QUESTIONNAIRE - ADULTS

Please read each item and decide if this is mostly true or mostly false for you. Circle the answer. Total your score by adding up number of true answers. The possible range of score is 0 to 22. Scores from 0 to 5 are considered normal, scores from 6 to 10 indicate a mild to moderate level of depression that is serous enough to interfere with your daily functioning. Scores of 11 and higher indicate a probable major depression with physical and psychological symptoms.

1. I gain little pleasure from anything   T   F
2. The things that used to make me happy don't do anymore T   F
3. Life is not really worth living most of time   T   F
4. My outlook is more gloomy than usual   T   F
5. I feel pretty hopeless about improving my life   T   F
6. I seem to have lost the ability to have any fun   T   F
7. I have been more unhappy than usual for at least a month T   F
8. I have been sleeping poorly for at least the last month   T   F
9. I have felt sad, down in the dumps, or blue much of the time during the last month   T   F
10. I have been more easily irritated or frustrated lately   T   F
11. I have cried or felt like crying more than twice during the last

month   T   F

12. I cry or feel saddened more easily than a few months ago   T   F

13. It is hard for me to get started on my daily chores and activities   T   F

14. I feel listless, tired, or fatigued a lot of the time   T   F

15. I feel worse in the morning than in the afternoon   T   F

16. I am definitely slowed down compared to my usual way of feeling   T   F

17. I have stopped several of my usual activities   T   F

18. I have regrets about the past that I think about often   T   F

19. My daily life is not interesting   T   F

20. I frequently feel like I don't care about anything anymore   T   F

21. My memory or thinking is not as good as usual   T   F

22. My appetite or digestion of food is worse than usual   T   F

Total number of "T" responses_____

*Adapted from Kemp, B and Adams, B. (1995) The Older Adults Health and Mood Questionnaire: A measure of geriatric depressive disorder. *Journal of Geriatric Psychiatry and Neurology, 8*(3), 162-167.

APPENDIX H: LIFE SATISFACTION QUESTIONNAIRE

Directions: Please rate your current satisfaction with these different parts of life. The scoring is as follows: **4=very satisfied, 3=mostly satisfied, 2=somewhat satisfied, 1=mostly dissatisfied.** Use NA if an area is not applicable.

1.	Physical Health............	1	2	3	4	NA
2.	Health Care...............	1	2	3	4	NA
3.	Emotional Health.......	1	2	3	4	NA
4.	Housing...................	1	2	3	4	NA
5.	Finances.................	1	2	3	4	NA
6.	Community Safety......	1	2	3	4	NA
7.	Leisure Activities.......	1	2	3	4	NA
8.	Career or Retirement....	1	2	3	4	NA
9.	Friendships................	1	2	3	4	NA
10.	Primary Relationship....	1	2	3	4	NA
11.	Family Relations..........	1	2	3	4	NA

Total Score_____

APPENDIX I: SOCIAL INTERACTION INVENTORY

Directions: Please indicate the **number of times in the last 7 days** that you did any of the following activities. If the answer is 'none', put in a '0'.

		Number
1.	Bought yourself something you wanted, a treat or gift for you.	_____
2.	Visited in person with a friend or friends.	_____
3.	Communicated on the phone or computer with a friend.	_____
4.	Went to a social event, like dinner or a party.	_____
5.	Had a romantic experience with someone.	_____
6.	Did anything fun.	_____
7.	Did something healthful for yourself.	_____
8.	Get out of the house.	_____
9.	Felt good about yourself when you were with other people.	_____
10.	Went shopping for other than food.	_____
11.	Talked to a neighbor.	_____

12. Went to the show, theater, concert, or sporting event. _____

13. Made plans to go on a trip, outing or to travel. _____

14. Dressed your best. _____

15. Went to church, synagogue, or temple _____

16. Went to any kind of group meeting. _____

TOTAL: _____

INDEX

Made in the USA
Lexington, KY
16 August 2013